SECULAR SANCTUARY

•

A Nonbeliever's Guide to Holy Moments and Sacred Spaces

By Carol Maher

Copyright ©2018 Carol Maher

All right reserved.

ISBN 978-0-692-16482-2

With thanks to
Denny, Jennifer, Jill, Julie, Marty,
and the HL Writing Group

"When you get, give;

when you learn, teach"

Maya Angelou

Dedicated to Warren

Contents

Introduction		*1*
Chapter One:	True Believer	4
Chapter Two:	Loss of Faith	17
Chapter Three:	Discovering the Holy	29
Chapter Four:	Establishing the Sanctuary	35
Chapter Five:	The Mystery of Spirit	48
Chapter Six:	Secular Morality	57
Chapter Seven:	Private Rites	70
Chapter Eight:	Shared Ceremonies	78

Introduction

If your faith in a supreme being who can and will break the laws of nature in answer to prayer is wavering, you are not alone. As science offers clearer understandings of our origins, and reveals how the universe works, many in the post-modern era find it impossible to continue to accept the pre-scientific explanations offered by religious teachings. Century upon century of evidence indicates that when we pray there's no one listening, ready, willing and able to intervene in the course of human or natural events. What once seemed unassailable truth now seems like superstition. Prayer may be unveiled as self-talk, or an effort to communicate with an imaginary, supernatural realm. At worst, prayer may seem like an attempt to unload personal responsibility onto an invisible surrogate. For many of us, the prayers, rituals and worldview we grew up with, grounded as they are in the supernatural, no longer speak to the world we find ourselves in today.

Our religions may no longer speak to us, but the cold hard facts of science are a poor substitute for the comforting assurances, communal life and all-embracing worldview of faith. When I realized that the religious doctrines I once upheld no longer made sense to me, and that the faith that had lived in me was dead, it seemed that the meaning and rhythm of life itself had drained away. It seemed that the earth was just a place where humans, like all living things, were born to suffer, eat, sleep, reproduce and die without purpose. Nothing mattered, and there was nothing worth celebrating. In my life there would be no more baptisms, weddings and funerals; no more prayers and hymns and holy days. And with no more God of Love, no more golden rule or ten commandments, how would I even know right from wrong?

I had always secretly pitied nonbelievers for what I imagined was the emptiness of their lives, with no god to thank in moments of joy or pray to in times of need, nor any heaven to hope for in death. It seemed to me that their lives must be devoid of sacred places and holy moments.

But my impression of the secular ("worldly") life was wrong. I have since learned that, quite apart from religion, the universe and the world we live in are overflowing with holiness. Not only this, but I have found that the human spirit is the source and origin of love; it is we who bless; it is you and I who set places, things and moments apart from a common to a sacred purpose. We consecrate the naming and welcoming of a baby. It is humans who mark the solemn joy of uniting a couple in marriage, and create the uplifting sense of wonder and hope when a dear one is laid to rest. There has never been any supernatural being present at these special moments: it has always been the power of the human spirit that has made them holy.

But of course, the ending of personal faith may be felt as a profound loss, and it is one that entails other losses as well. Especially if you once belonged to a community of shared belief, then you may now also be suffering the emptiness of losing that camaraderie, or at least feeling a new distance between you and those familiar faces. This has been one of the hardest parts of leaving the church for me and I still remember the fellowship halls I have known, filled with chatting, laughing friends and running children. But does losing a community of faith mean that that there will be no more occasions to gather with friends over coffee and cookies? Truly, it does not.

My long history in the church as member, officer and minister of word and sacrament means that I find it hard to use words like spirit, sacred, holy, altar and sanctuary in reference to human experience. And yet because these words have been so well crafted through generations of use to point to the ineffable realms of spiritual experience, I find that they remain the most suitable words for speaking of those experiences even without divine reference. I now understand that a place or thing becomes sacred for me when I set it aside from a common to a spiritual purpose, and that the time I spend in communion with my spirit is a holy moment because I have blessed it. The place where I take time for spirit, and the surface within it upon which I place symbols of my inner being are my sanctuary and my altar.

When speaking of that mysterious human energy that is neither thought nor emotion I use the word spirit. Impossible to fully understand, perhaps we may still ask whether this human spark might be our individual allotment from the energy that powers the whole universe, and whether we are able to commune with that larger energy in meditation. Our body is always busy with thoughts and emotions, sensations, drives, itches, pains and pleasures. Can it be that this constant activity is all that distracts us from experiencing the spirit within and around us? Is it possible to calm the body sufficiently in meditation so that spirit may emerge? And further, could it be that the energy of the universe is seeking to re-gather its scattered sparks, and in so doing, is drawing humans to each other in love and mutual responsibility? Is love an elemental force of nature, expressed through the human spirit? I believe all of these things may be so.

With new, secular understandings of these words in mind, perhaps you can join me in embracing the holiness of your own life, the sacredness of the world, and the power of your own spirit, allowing these terms to stand on their own without religious baggage.

Chapter One: True Believer

In the churches of my childhood, children didn't question what they were taught, but rather we did our best to learn it by heart. Every lesson, every song, every ritual, rite and sacrament was designed to hold together as a system in which every part logically supports every other part. Together it all made perfect sense. If you followed the rules, you would be rewarded on earth and in heaven: your parents would praise you, you would do well in school, friends would invite you to birthday parties, and God would love you. If you were bad, your parents would scold and punish, your teacher might embarrass you, you would lose friends, and worst of all, God would put a black mark next to your name in his Big Book. In the Sunday nursery we were taught this song:

> *Oh, be careful little hands what you do;*
> *Oh, be careful little tongue what you say;*
> *Oh, be careful little ears where you hear;*
> *Oh, be careful little feet where you go;*
> *For the Father up above is looking down with love;*
> *So be careful....*

Shame, and an almost paranoiac sense of a ghostly presence watching our every move, kept us all in line at church, and even made me fearful when I was alone. I was sure God was always looking over my shoulder and passing judgement on everything I said and did, so I was very, very careful. But I was also secure in my belief that The Father Up Above saw my obedience, and my obedience would be rewarded. Life made sense. There were commandments and laws and elders to obey, and friends to love. I worked hard to learn my lessons and follow the rules, to be prepared, and to be a friend to every Girl Scout.

But then, as it happened, one of my friends at church, an angelic little girl named Gloria, was diagnosed with leukemia. She endured a prolonged and painful death over a period of many months. When our Sunday School class paid her a visit, I was deeply moved by her thin body and vacant eyes. But when I looked into the faces of her grief-wracked parents I was struck by the injustice of it all. This was a good family who attended church every Sunday and gave generously of their time and talents. And yet it seemed that they were being punished by God. Our Sunday School class prayed for Gloria every week, and I prayed for her at home, alone in my bed. We all begged God to make her well.

And yet, Gloria died not long after our class visit. Clearly our fervent prayers, and the prayers of the whole church, had not been answered. But we were told by our teacher that in fact our prayers had been answered, because Gloria's suffering had ended. We were assured that God, in his love, had prepared a home for her in heaven where she would never be sick again. We were told that God works in mysterious ways, and that it was wrong to question his wisdom.

I accepted this admonition since, of course God knows best, and he arranges things according to his long-range plans, which are impossible for us to comprehend. And thus the "inscrutability of the will of God" became the foundational unprovable, and therefore unquestionable, tenet of my young faith. God might be everywhere at once, know everything, be all-loving and all-powerful, but it would never be possible to understand how, when or why he would use those powers. So don't ask.

I was twelve when I took Membership Confirmation Classes at my church. We were a big baby-boomer class, probably thirty kids around the table in Fellowship Hall every Saturday morning for eight weeks. We memorized the books of the Bible, the Apostles' Creed, the Westminster Confession and some of the Westminster Catechism. Everywhere, the doctrine of salvation from the depravity of original sin by the grace of God through faith in the crucified and risen Christ was expressed, sometimes as a theological abstraction, sometimes in gory detail. According to this doctrine, even Gloria's sins had to be washed away in Christ's blood so she could qualify for the home God had prepared for her in heaven. Gloria had been only seven at the time of her death, and, according to experts in the field of human moral development, incapable of sin. The doctrine of original sin as it was being presented to me seemed to slander the good character of the innocent girl I had known.

Furthermore, according to these teachings, salvation is granted to believing Christians by the grace of God alone, and cannot be earned. Our efforts to follow the commandments and live according to God's will cannot save us. On the other hand, it seems that we can lose our salvation and be damned to eternal punishment if we disobey God's laws. And the final insult to both mercy and common sense is given in the doctrine of predestination, according to which the saving grace of God is granted, not even to all believers, but only to a select few among them whom God chose "before time."

That meant that everyone who was not a confessing Christian, plus some who were, would be sent to hell by the very God who had created them in his image. What seemed to stand between most of the population of the world and eternal life with their Creator was a gate keeper named Jesus, and I had a bone to pick with him.

After Confirmation Class one Saturday I asked to speak privately with the minister. In his office I confessed my suspicion that I might be Jewish instead of Christian. "I just don't see any reason for Jesus," I told him. "I get the part about him coming to earth to show us how to live. But why did God need him to die on the cross to let us into heaven? Why can't God accept us without that?"

The minister was visibly annoyed. He assured me that I was not Jewish and that I still had a lot to learn. Everything would become clear as I got older. But for now, I shouldn't worry about such things.

And so, for six more years, I didn't.

At our church, Youth Sunday was celebrated with a parade of children, from littlest to biggest, down the center aisle of the sanctuary. The youngest children were given a pansy in a cup of dirt to take home and plant. The older children received promotion certificates and attendance award pins. And one graduating senior was selected to deliver that Sunday's sermon. The year I graduated from high school, that senior was me.

I remember my sermon title: "The Untested Faith." As I looked forward to college, I told the congregation that it's easy to express your faith by just repeating what you've been told when you live with people who believe as you do. But it will become more difficult to hold onto those beliefs when you go out into the world and meet people who think differently, and who challenge your beliefs. When that happens, I told my well-travelled and time-tested elders, you will find out whether the truth of what you believe actually lives in you as an abiding faith, or whether your beliefs are merely a recitation of ideas you have been taught.

Everyone thought my sermon was wonderful, my parents were proud, and I was absolutely certain my faith was strong enough to meet any test. As it turned out, and quite appropriately, my first college roommate was agnostic and she challenged me every day. She thought I was hopelessly naive and rolled her eyes when I argued for the existence of God from the "evidence" of Scripture. Her reasoning was flawless and I struggled to keep up my end of the daily disputes.

That fall I began dating a history major named Denny. He also turned out to be agnostic, so I was hearing the same things and fighting the same battle in the dorm and on my dates. But since I was beginning to fall in love with this guy, I listened with great interest to everything he said, from his convictions on the Russian revolution to the impossibility of the existence of a supernatural god. I found his worldview fascinating and his logic compelling.

I remember the day it all clicked for me. I was alone in the dorm room when I accepted the idea that I had been misled in my beliefs. I didn't occur to me then that the loss of my faith was something to grieve, as I do now. All I saw was freedom. And following immediately upon that realization came the insight that, if there was no god, then I had no moral compass. The ten commandments, heaven and hell, and the teachings of the church had no power over me. I saw no more reason to resist the urgings of love. That night after dinner, I put on my coat and walked from the dorm across town to Denny's apartment and climbed into his bed.

Our love deepened over the following months and we were engaged that spring. We planned a traditional midsummer church wedding to satisfy our parents. Just weeks before our wedding, while I was still living in the dorm, I received news that my only brother had been killed in a car accident. He and Denny had been high school friends, and so the two of us faced his death with no god to comfort us, and no hope of heaven.

During the following year I experienced a profound longing to return to my faith. It was not only because I needed to believe that my brother was safely in heaven, but also because I was for the first time viscerally aware that I, too, would end up under the earth. Shivering terrors overtook me at the awful prospect, and I began wandering into churches on my lunch breaks. Sitting in the front pew,

I would stare up at the cross and mentally cry out for divine help.

On our next visit home, I asked my father why I couldn't find God. I explained my longing and told him about my fruitless visits to the sanctuaries. Using an old hunting term, Dad said I was trying too hard to find God and was "overshooting the mark." He told me that God was always already within me, closer than my own breath.

In the desperation of my need, and in the living presence of my father's simple trust, I found that my doubts vanished and my old unquestioning, blind faith was restored. Wasn't this exactly the testing I had spoken of on Youth Sunday, and hadn't I come through it with flying colors! With a rush of relief I knew that I could pray again, and that God would receive me into heaven when I died as he had certainly received my brother, and that I needn't worry anymore about the demise of my body, nor of my brother's.

It does seem strange that it all came back so easily. At the time I credited the power of the Holy Spirit at work in me to restore what was broken. I now believe that it was my own spirit at work in me to restore what was broken. My faith in God had always been grounded in a decision to accept the teachings of the church. That decision had been made for me at my baptism. I had chosen it for myself in Confirmation, and in that moment with Dad, I chose it yet again.

But for my young husband in those days it was not so easy. Denny wanted to join me in faith but had a longer history outside of the church than in it. He had no habits of prayer or worship. On the suggestion of the pastor of the church we began attending, he set himself the task of reading the four Gospels straight through, from the beginning of Matthew to the end of John. And as he did this, his heart went out to Jesus. We joined the church and got involved in outreach ministries to the homeless in Chicago. It was then that he experienced a sense of call to professional ministry. We lived near McCormick Presbyterian Theological Seminary. He applied and was accepted and three years later, began his career as Minister of Word and Sacrament.

With his ministry, the role of minister's wife fell to me. I basked in the reflected glory of his title. There were occasions when I was deeply envious of the position he held in the church and in the community. A call to serve in ministry had burned in me for most of my life, and it was sometimes hard to stand back and let him be the one who led the people in prayer. The words he used were not always the words I would have chosen. His sermons seemed too political to me, and his sacraments and ceremonies not spiritual enough. I longed to fulfill my own faith as a professional servant of the Word.

In 1995, in my late forties, the pressure of my own call became irresistible. We were living near Louisville, Kentucky, at the time as Denny worked in the denominational headquarters. At the end of our first year there we attended a convention of church governing body leaders. The keynote speaker challenged the group to lead the church back to its original calling as followers of the radical justice of Jesus. I was deeply moved as I realized that it was not too late for me to answer the call. The opportunity lay before me to step up and do what I could to move the church forward as clergy rather than as an active Elder.

When I entered Louisville Presbyterian Theological Seminary that summer, I wasn't naive about scripture. I was married to a liberal minister, and had looked at many of his seminary textbooks. I had debated some fine points of theology with his clergy friends. I entered already knowing that the gospel is a truth that transcends the words that carry it.

But I was unprepared for the kind of brutal, detailed biblical criticism my professors engaged in. In the first semester, many of the more evangelical students dropped out, unable to accept the reality of the Bible as a haphazardly constructed and loosely substantiated anthology. As some of my favorite passages were picked apart or shown to be borrowed entirely from Sumerian or Egyptian or Persian texts, I figured these first critiques must be like removing flaking paint from the surface of a solid piece of furniture: at some point we would get down to solid wood. But layer after layer was peeled away until nothing remained except the shadow of the possibility of stories heard about visions that might have been revealed to someone, somewhere, long ago.

Can faith hold without scriptural underpinnings? I was finding that the Bible does not bear up well under very close scrutiny, and totally blind faith is impossible. My faith in the invisible spirit of God just barely held, but my system of belief was reduced to a logical use of the literature of Scripture, and a fine-tuned appreciation for the forms of worship and government of our denomination.

Somehow, I graduated at the top of my class, and was singled out for recognition in several academic areas. Even so, I had a hard time finding a church as a fifty year old woman with no pulpit experience beyond a student apprenticeship. Denny and I circulated our dossiers at the same time and he found work first, so we moved to Peoria, Illinois, the location of his next position. I was discouraged but knew the church well enough to realize that my best chances lay with the smaller, rural congregations which were abundant in the area. I began doing pulpit supply while continuing to look for a permanent position.

Eventually a church in the southern part of the state invited me to lead a Sunday service and sit for an interview. After the service a woman on the search committee said to me, "You preached that we can read the Bible with the same creativity in which it was written. I found that kind of shocking. Don't you believe that God dictated every word of scripture? Isn't it the Word of God, just as it's written, without any need for interpretation? Doesn't every word of the Bible govern your daily living?"

I remember thinking that my answer would determine my fate with this church, but I did not want to start off with a lie, so I said slowly, "No, but....," and as I began to offer my explanation of the Living Word, she burst into tears and fled from the room. As others went after her, some stayed to explain to me that her husband had just died and that the Bible was all that was holding her together.

Another rural church did end up calling me and I served them from 1999 through 2003. The town had fewer than two thousand residents and the church was made up of around eighty people, mostly undereducated farmers. I made many similar mistakes there, and always for the same reason: I didn't want to perpetuate among them the same belief in the infallibility of Scripture that had been taught to me. It's possible that, without being aware of it, I looked down on their narrow views. I only know that I hoped that, by challenging them to read the words of scripture with an open heart and mind, I might be an invigorating influence.

But they did not welcome the opportunity to think creatively about Scripture, nor did they want to acknowledge the pharisaic legalism they enforced in their homes, churches and fraternal orders in the name of God. They didn't welcome my teaching, and those who caught a glimpse of the freedom I was talking about began a whispering campaign to force my resignation. Officials of the regional church governing body were called in to "facilitate a dialogue."

It came to a bitter end, and my leaving that small church coincided with Denny also having to change jobs. The denominational job market was tightening and in moving on we both turned to "interim" ministry, he in church administration, and I continuing in pastoral ministry.

I still was not fully aware that my faith in God was falling apart. This was probably because the God I believed in was defined entirely by the Bible, which I now viewed with deep skepticism, but which consumed my every working hour as I struggled to draw a sermon out of one passage or another: it was truly a case of not seeing the forest for the trees. I thought I was still preaching well, and delivering a strong spiritual message. And most of all I still believed that, when properly read and preached, scripture could be a pathway through which the Holy Spirit could enliven the church.

The job of the interim minister is to work herself out of a job, shepherding a congregation through the process of searching for and calling a permanent minister. As each position ended I sought another church, and ended up serving three more for about one year each. As it turned out, one year was just long enough in each setting for a whispering campaign to begin against me as a heretic and a radical. There were always a few who realized before the others that I was not a biblical literalist, that I did not believe in the young earth, that I did not accept the creation stories, nor believe in the actual existence of Adam and Eve, or Noah and Jonah.

All I can say on my behalf is that I didn't lie to them. Instead I felt duty-bound to invite them to join me in listening beyond the words of scripture for the voice of the Spirit of God.

While I was serving my fourth and last church, my father died. He died during the week before Easter and my sister, who had lived next door to Dad and cared for him during the last years of his life, wanted to have the funeral on the Saturday before Easter. I was still deluding myself that I was a good, though often misunderstood, minister and that my congregation would not do well if I left them with a stranger -- or worse, with no clergy -- to lead them in worship on Easter Sunday. I was in New York and my sister was in Missouri. I promised her that I would come for the burial on Monday, but I would stay in New York to lead Easter worship.

When I mentioned in my Easter sermon the story of the man who was traveling with Jesus but wanted to take time to go home and bury his father, and when I reminded them that Jesus had told this man that if he did that he would not be worthy of the kingdom, and when I further said that it was because of that story that I was with them instead of at my father's funeral -- I did not sense warm appreciation from the congregation. The whispering campaign was already in high gear, and very soon the pastoral search committee had settled on my replacement.

As the members filed past me to say goodbye on my last Sunday, one of the elders leaned in to whisper in my ear. In my sadness I longed for a reminder of the friendship we had shared. But instead of saying, "I will miss you," she whispered, "I forgive you." And with that, the last shred of my faith in the spirit of God, even as the tie that binds the church, fell away.

That same week I moved in with Denny in another city where he was serving out the last months of an interim call. During those few months, with no hope at the age of 60 for finding another church, I finally realized where I was theologically. Now that there was no longer anyone to impress, I could admit the truth to myself: I no longer believed in God and had no reason to pretend that I did. My life in the church was really over.

Chapter Two: Loss of Faith

Faith, like love, is blind.

If you no longer believe in the god you once worshiped and no longer find acceptable the teachings that once guided your life, then your eyes are open in a way they have not been before. You are seeing the object of your devotion clearly for the first time, and must now decide whether to close your eyes again and recommit, or to keep them open and move into a new way, a new truth, and a new life. That happened to me, and perhaps you'll find something of your own story in mine.

It was not only the undercutting of the authority of scripture in seminary, or the absence of spirit I encountered in the churches, but also my own recognition of the futility of continuing a one-sided relationship with an imaginary figure, that caused me to finally give up the ghost. One of my favorite Bible School songs was based on a passage from the Gospels. The song goes:

> *Behold, behold, I stand at the door and*
> > *knock, knock knock!*
> *If anybody hears my voice let them*
> > *open, open, open the door, I will come in!*

We sang it with gusto, pounding on our chairs and stamping our feet to make the loudest knocking noises we could, and then opening our arms wide and wider to welcome Jesus. And so, with early training and happy memories like this, it was with some sadness that I set aside that childlike trust as an adult, and admitted that there's no one on the other side of the door.

Except you. You are the one knocking. And I am the one knocking on your door. I have allowed an imagined relationship with a fictitious savior to stand in for a real relationship with you, my stranger and neighbor. I can't help wondering what I have missed, what I have lost, and how I have failed to be there for the real people in my world, while I was preoccupied with the paper people of the bible? It's true, there is fellowship in the church, but looking back, it was a closed and judgmental sort of community.

When I opened my eyes at the age of sixty and saw that the God I had known and loved was nothing more than a beautiful and all-encompassing myth, I saw also how much time, energy, talent, and money I had spent serving the myth. And not only I, but it seemed the whole world had gone mad for this story. Was I the only one who saw through it? For a while it was the enormity of the worldwide church and its evangelistic fervor through history that held me in most strongly. A narrative this large and lasting could not possibly be false, could it?

In the end, common sense won over wishful thinking and I left god in the bible for others to struggle with. I was through and could not go back. My eyes were open, and I preferred sight to blindness.

But of course, what I saw at first seemed to lack the dramatic purpose and daily magic of the beliefs I had been living. In the absence of god the world seemed foreign and oddly mechanical. I experienced a nagging and complex grief. The loss felt like a death. Not the shock of an accidental death as had befallen my brother, but more like the death of Santa Claus after a long period of quietly held suspicions. But still, it hurt: I had lost the ruler of my heart, my oldest and dearest friend, truest mentor, most beloved parent, and the highest moral authority I could imagine.

I had lost a family tie, too, since this was the faith that my father had cherished, and had been the fortress and foundation of my grandmothers. But they were all dead, and I was grateful, at least, not to have to explain myself to any of them.

Along with cutting that tie to my real family, in losing my faith I also cut ties with my church family, losing a lifelong network of social connections. A barrier had risen between myself and almost everyone I had ever known, shutting me off from the fellowship of countless relatives, friends, work groups, governing bodies, from the projects and the meals we had shared, the deep discussions, and the fun we had had. I knew I could never again, in good conscience, sit through a worship service or bow my head during public prayer. I knew my views would not be well received among any of the folks I had known, and it suddenly occurred to me that I could be excommunicated or defrocked, and even lose my church pension (although neither happened). Not only was I bereft, I also felt betrayed, and began to resent those who had trained me to accept traditions without question. Worst of all, I felt ashamed of myself as as institutional leader and purveyor of that mythology.

My world of meaning, which had been filled with sacred spaces and holy moments, had fallen apart. From the day of my birth, my life had been scheduled around the sabbaths and seasons of the church. I had been moved by the beauty and peace of sanctuaries, stirred by solemn rites of passage, and transported by symbolic objects and words. My aesthetic intelligence had been stretched through the glory of sacred music, poetry, stories of heroes and villains, brave men and women and journeys of transformation, ancient and modern art, and pageantry. Every walk in the woods, every waterfall and lake, every sunset and sunrise, every birth and death, all had spoken of the glory and power of god and been wrapped in praise and thanksgiving. I feared that, with the loss of faith, beauty itself would be closed off from me.

Until then I had tamed my wildest fears and sorrows by giving them to god in prayer. Until then my helplessness in the face of need had been turned to good purpose, or so I thought, in the act of prayer. And until then, my fear of death had been eased in the assurance that when my time came, god would call me home, and I would simply rise and go.

All of these joys and comforts and connections were now lost. When I truly realized that my life with god and my life in the church were over, I wept and worried and journaled alone for many months. During that time Denny and I moved again, and I briefly lost track of my grief in the tangle of setting up a new home. But when it resurfaced with new force, I decided to throw my grief out to the world in the form of a question. In the search window I typed, "Grieving the loss of my faith," and hit return. Seconds later, to my surprise, out poured a seemingly endless list of people and websites to visit. Many, many others, it seems, were struggling with the same dilemma I was facing, and I began to read.

You, too, may find the internet approach helpful. In spite of its invasive ads and complex connections, the world wide web can be a source of inspiration and enlightenment. In phrasing your initial question, be as specific as you can. Refine your question according to the results that come up and see what happens. Whether or not you choose to use the internet to find fellow seekers, I assure you that you are not alone in your quest for renewal. Use common sense, though: don't give out personal information or agree to meet with anyone you don't know.

One of the first places I clicked on was a blog called "The Friendly Atheist," and this turned out to be a good first move because it led me to other avenues of inquiry. Here is the letter I wrote under the pseudonym "Barbara," followed by Richard Wade's response.

> *PATHEOS.COM/BLOGS/THEFRIENDLYATHEIST*
> ***ASK RICHARD: "Former Minister Grieves the Loss of Her Faith"***
> *JANUARY 2, 2012 BY RICHARD WADE*
> *Note: Letter writers' names are changed for privacy.*

Dear Richard,

Thank you for being there (in "The Friendly Atheist") when I finally realized I was grieving the loss of my faith. After a lifetime of service to the Presbyterian Church, culminating in seminary and pastoral ministry, my belief in God left me completely three years ago, at the end of a difficult interim position. I'm 64 years old. My husband, also clergy, never took anything in scripture literally and often ridiculed my beliefs. Now I find myself even farther out than he is. I also did a Master's in existential philosophy (before seminary) and see no point in mental gymnastics. I watched my dad, a great and learned man, lose his mind during the years before his actual death. Nothing lasts, why strive? You advocate something called "secular humanism." I always saw that as the enemy of Christianity so I know nothing. What's it about and what's good in it? Ayn Rand is about the extent of my knowledge and I found her horribly egotistical. I'm sad except when I'm with my granddaughter and the three or four women I volunteer with. I'm not suicidal, although I don't see any grand purpose in life or living.

Sincerely,
Barbara

P.S. I just occurred to me that for the first time I'm grateful for (instead of angry about) the secularization of Christmas as I still enjoy the gifting and decorating.

Dear Barbara,

I think you're still in the midst of your grieving. The greater the importance that a cherished person, thing or commitment has for us, the greater the grief we suffer when it passes away from us. Grief can last quite a while, and it fades away gradually. Your commitment was enormous, and so I'm not surprised if after three years you are still mourning.

What you are describing also sounds a little like depression, which sometimes accompanies grief, but which can settle in and become chronic, remaining even after the grief is over. I'm glad that you reassure us that you're not suicidal, but it also might be good for you to run through the main items on the depression checklist. While grief for any kind of loss can have many of the traits here, they generally taper off over time. For depression, look for a pattern of persistence or even increase over time:

- *Feeling daily sad, empty, purposeless, worthless, helpless, hopeless, or inappropriately guilty.*
- *Irritability, impatience, anxiety.*
- *Loss of interest in friends, family, hobbies, pleasurable things.*
- *Difficulty concentrating, remembering things, or making decisions.*
- *Changes in appetite, significant weight loss not from dieting, or weight gain.*
- *Loss of energy, fatigue, moving very slowly.*
- *Insomnia or excessive sleeping.*
- *Unexplained physical symptoms, such as headaches, stomach aches, body pains.*
- *Recurring thoughts of death or suicide, wishing to die.*

If you have any of these to a significant level, or if you have some of these to a moderate level, I think you should consult a doctor or counselor or both. If you decide that therapy would be helpful, be certain that it is not pastoral counseling in any form. Regular, secular, psychology-based counseling would be the best choice for you.

Aside from that issue, it sounds like your loss of faith also resulted in a loss of things for you to do. The timing of this in your sixties, when not only are you adjusting to changes in your body, you're also adjusting to changes in roles that you and society might expect of you. This could be adding to your sense of being adrift and directionless.

Seeking a direction, you asked about humanism. Descriptions and definitions differ, but I think that you can get a good understanding from the material on the **American Humanist Association** *website. Read all of the essays on that page, not just the Humanist Manifesto. For someone with a Master's in existential philosophy, these should be easy reading. Ayn Rand is probably not the best representative of what humanism can be. Here I ask our very learned Friendly Atheist readers out there for their recommendations for further reading on humanism....*

You need some peers, some people who understand what you are going through because they have been there too. The internet is a wonderful tool for this, and a few online atheist friends who can recognize exactly what you share are very important. Again, I ask our readers if they know of good sources for former clergy to find each other. Finally, former clergy or not, having at least one trusted atheist friend with whom you can meet face to face is invaluable. Keep looking, don't give up.

I don't pretend to understand much about existentialism, but I do remember that Jean-Paul Sartre said, "Man is nothing else but what he makes of himself." You can choose your own purpose, invent whatever meaning you wish for your life, cast yourself in whatever role you please.... It's deeply and wonderfully all yours. Judging from your letter, I think your role will have much to do with helping other people.

You asked, "Nothing lasts, so why strive?" I reply, "Yes, nothing lasts, so strive!" Make the most of this limited time. Don't live inconsequentially, have an effect! Leave the world a little better because you were here. It might not be a grand and famous difference you'll make in the world as a whole, but it can be grand and famous in the lives of those people who are lucky enough to know you.

You're already on the right track by spending time being happy with your granddaughter and the three or four women with whom you volunteer. Ah, volunteering. You're already practicing an important expression of humanism. You'll find from your reading and your own experience that other human beings are both the essence and the embodiment of humanism, the essence and embodiment of your own humanity. Expand your love, your caring, your willingness, your interaction, your positive effect on others, and you expand your own life.

Richard

As you might imagine, I did recognize in myself some of those signs of depression, and I soon located a good counselor. But in fact it was a reader's response to my letter to Richard that did the most to lift me out of the darkness. She directed me to a secret online group of former clergy -- priests, nuns, rabbis, ministers, chaplains, pastors and pastoral counselors -- who had recently come to atheism. After rigorous screening, including two in-person phone calls, I was granted access to the group. I was inexperienced with chat room protocols and at first found it confusing, as many threads of conversation were already in progress covering a wide range of topics. But the spirit of the group was one of such optimism that I kept on reading the stories of others, and telling my own. Secular resources were freely shared as we all endeavored to find new meaning in situations that had once belonged entirely to God and church. I will be forever in debt to Richard Wade for his generous answer to my letter, and to the courageous former clergy in that chat room who invited me to believe in myself, and in the possibility of a meaningful and holy life without god.

Whatever the form or degree of your involvement in religion, you will certainly find others online and elsewhere who are also grieving the loss of faith and would be most grateful to hear your story and tell you theirs.

•

Big grief is a gift that keeps on giving. Just when you start thinking that you've moved on and let it go, you may discover a whole new level.

I was looking back into work I had done for church groups over the years, thinking that with a few language changes some of the liturgies and retreats I had written might be useful in a secular setting. The first folder I opened was labeled "Praying with our Feet," and I remembered the women's association who had commissioned me to write it. They wanted to spend a weekend doing visioning and preparation before launching into a new mission year.

As I looked over the handwritten sheet of reminders I had prepared for the event, I thought, "This is pretty good!" I had included in the retreat a bowl-and-pitcher foot washing ceremony recalling both Jesus' ministry to his disciples and Mary Magdalen's ministry to him, and also plans for labyrinth walks with a guiding question.

But when I began to read the actual manuscript for the weekend, my blood ran cold. I shut the folder and began to weep. I had the feeling that I had just glimpsed the dead body of someone I loved. It was beautiful, and it had been written in the power of the holy spirit, a spirit which I no longer believed in. I felt that I would never write that well again, nor that creatively, since the power behind my pen was gone. The grief I thought had passed returned with force, and filled me with longing. Seeing my confident advice to the women, and remembering the faith in which it had been offered, brought back a memory of my sense of the constant protection of god. Here was the very epicenter of my loss, and my heart broke all over again.

As I sat on the floor surrounded by folders and photocopies, I was reminded of sitting with my sister in the same way among our mother's things after her death. In my sadness I had thought that I would keep nothing, because the presence of her things in my home would only remind me of her absence. In that same way, as I looked at my labors spread around me, I felt that I could not use anything from this retreat or from the countless other things I'd written for the church. They had been written in a power that was now dead to me, and their use would only remind me of that enormous absence.

And then I heard one of my mother's own sayings, "Don't throw the baby out with the bath water!"

In fact, my sister and I chose well among Mom's things, and to this day I enjoy many of her kitchen tools, including her wooden recipe box. So I picked up my work again and, reminding myself that I had not, in fact, been writing "in the power of" any supernatural force since no such force exists, I reread it with a new determination to discern the actual source of its undeniable power.

For some reason, as I read, my thoughts turned to the Disney animated film "Dumbo," in which a baby circus elephant finds that he is able to fly, and believes that he is able to do so because of the feather he holds in his trunk. Disney had an eye for the power of myth, and this story sends a universal message when we learn that Dumbo did not need the feather, but had always been able to fly by virtue of his enormous ears (of which he had been made to feel ashamed). He discovers this native ability when, in a long dive from a tower, the feather slips from his grip, yet he soars away and out of the circus tent.

It might sound silly, but it was in the lesson of Dumbo that I saw what had happened in the retreat in a new way. In preparing and leading it, I had called upon an imaginary holy spirit in the belief that I needed it to bring spiritual power into my work. And yet it had been my own spirit, reaching in to the depths of my soul and out toward communion with others, that had infused the event with spiritual power. In the work of preparation I had been transported on the wings of my own spirit, and as I invited the participants to enter into spiritual play, they found their wings and rose to meet me. We found that we were able to fly on our own, and together we created a sacred setting and a holy moment infused with spiritual energy.

The good that remained in the retreat, after throwing out the god-language and holy spirit references, was the fact that a group of women had become a spiritual community, at least for a weekend. Together we had consecrated a space, and lived into a holy moment without help from beyond. The holiness of the community, the place and the moment may not have outlived the event, but while it lasted it shimmered with the holy vitality of the human spirit.

The grief of disillusionment is terrible. You may find that it feels more like you've been betrayed by a loved one and abandoned by friends, than that you've misunderstood something. With this feeling of betrayal may come a sense of having been duped, and this may carry with it a load of embarrassment and shame. If your faith was strong, this is a complex grief that does not pass quickly. There will be a period of emptiness as teachings once held dear lose their force and new understandings are not yet clear. On the other hand, if your belief in god was more tentative, and your connections to a religious community were minimal, you may be ready to move on unburdened by a strong sense of loss.

Life is inherently holy. The weight of religious tradition meets its match in the power of the human spirit. Life is good, the soul is resilient, and still greater truths are waiting to be discovered.

Chapter Three: Discovering the Holy

The ancient questions that originally gave rise to the human acts of imagining gods and making superstitions are finding real answers in the sciences. There is much to celebrate in these discoveries. People who have moved beyond faith are welcoming these new perspectives and doing what they can to bring them into view. There is opportunity here for all of us to build on new truths to create a world in which the human spirit is celebrated in itself, without reference to an imagined spiritual realm. Although much good has been done in the name of religion, much harm has been done, as well. We are free today to choose among all that is good in all of the social systems and religions of the world to redefine the moral life, and create new structures of mutual understanding, shared responsibility, and justice.

Paul Muller-Ortega observes in his *Tantra Meditation* series that we live in an "awakening time," a time of global cultural convergence in which there is a rising awareness that, beyond the visible, there is more. He likens our time to the moment when "night is over, but the sun is not yet risen." People are seeking new ways of knowing, and finding resources in world religious practices. And today, he notes, all of this is available on the internet. This ready access to all that is, or ever has been, considered sacred in the world has been of enormous help to me in my journey, and I believe my readings have even influenced my dreams.

I woke from a dream this morning in which I had experienced remarkable powers. I lay awake recalling great strength, carrying weapons, running, leaping and wearing gold armor. I waited to see if some meaning would emerge. And it did seem that in the dream I had been a god, and I marveled at how much being a god had seemed like being human. Then it hit me that all gods, even the biblical god I had worshiped, were like that: they were all projections of human characteristics. There was nothing attributed to a god that was not first part of being human. The gods had not made us in their image, we had made them in our image! And in imagining our gods, we had endowed them with the characteristics we knew best, and ascribed to them our virtues, elevated to the highest degree.

I saw that to be human is to be the source of all godly powers, the very origin and model of everything that is good and strong and holy. I saw that we ourselves already possess everything we have ever considered sacred. I suddenly saw being human is a kind of miracle, a gift, a challenge, and life's highest calling. But it also struck me that I was a human who had willed away her powers.

And it seemed to me that, as my belief in the reality of the created gods died away, the powers I had projected from myself onto them remained, suspended, as it were, in space. They were not gone, but waiting for me to reclaim them. They were my own human powers to begin with, and they are mine to have once again. I realized that we are the ones who bless, and the blessing comes from us. We are the ones who sanctify, and the sacredness that is given is ours to bestow.

But I could see also that human powers entrusted to gods do not return as soon as belief in the gods ends. For a time those powers are truly lost from the self, and a sense of powerlessness is experienced. I realized also that I would not be able to reclaim anything until I could name what I had given away.

As I considered these things I realized that I had to face the hard truth that the god into whose open hands I had willingly poured my strength and life was nothing more than a cardboard cutout, a false front which concealed an infinite void. I confessed to myself and knew it was true that this god-image had been placed there by others but had been kept there by me, to protect myself from seeing and knowing the void, the shoreless sea, the infinite unknown.

The great news of the dream, the news that made me smile into my pillow, was that all of the human powers and attributes I had given away as offerings to the cardboard god had passed through, as sweet dreams pass through the center of a dream catcher. They were not lost, but there in the void. And I wanted them back. I wanted them so that I might be restored to my self. Did I have the courage to go after them?

In my imagination I continued the story of the dream and tore away the cardboard god. It was shabby and loose and fell apart easily. Behind it I encountered first, not the void itself, but my child-self looking up at me, with her back to the void.

"Don't go there," she begged. "I'm afraid."

I lifted her into my arms and held her close, saying, "Don't be afraid. I'll be with you."

As I gazed into the terrible darkness, out from it stepped an old woman who I knew at once was the grandmother of all of my grandmothers. She opened her arms and enfolded us both, saying, "Fear not. I will be with you."

So I entered the void in the shelter of my grandmother's arms and with a frightened child in my heart, only to find that I had come into familiar territory! Here I was in the mystery of my own inner being, among the shadows and intuitions that have awakened awe in my soul, the fears that have haunted me, the devastating prospect of nonbeing, and the blinding light of truths too large to comprehend. Here also were the powers I had given up, every one of them, and here was courage to claim them. All of these things were mine.

•

At first, and for a while, it may seem to you that you'll never know what you've lost in attributing your finest characteristics and greatest powers to the god you believed in.

But in fact it's possible to reconstruct the entire package by remembering how you used to describe your god. What powers, qualities, and virtues did you ascribe to him or her? Those powers, qualities and virtues are parts of yourself. You made this god in your own image, and you will find there, in all that you ascribed to him or her, everything that rightfully belongs to you.

This does not mean that you are a god, or that any of us could become a god even if we were somehow able to embody all of the powers once ascribed to a supernatural being. Gods are imaginary creatures. We are human, and that is more than enough. The point is that these great characteristics already belong to us, and their names represent the highest forms of integrity, strength and virtue that humans can hope for. Of course, no one ever fully embodies all of the great human qualities we have used to describe our gods. For now it is enough that we are able to name them, and that we claim the authority by which they belong to us. For now, simply know that these strengths and virtues do not exist outside of you somewhere, but rather within you as your own-most potential.

As I recalled the image of the god I once worshiped, I made a list of the powers and virtues I had ascribed to him, and which I am now endeavoring to reclaim as my own.

Love: I was taught to say, "God is love," and this is perhaps the deepest cut of all. Love is the highest attainment of the human spirit. In all the universe, human love is the one completely uncaused and unpredictable force of nature. In spite of Heisenberg's *Uncertainty Principle*, every action does have a cause, whether or not we can trace it. But love isn't caused, it's freely given. It acts in illogical ways, without discernible reason, running toward danger, outstripping its own strength, giving itself away for the sake of the beloved. It's the holiest thing there is about being human and therefore it's understandable that in creating a holy god, we would make the god's name interchangeable with love. But there' nothing supernatural about love. It is quintessentially human, and our greatest gift.

Righteousness: In the marvelously evolved human brain, reason and emotion work together to give us the ability to evaluate our own behavior and the behavior of others. We judge what is good from our own experience of pleasure, and what is bad from our experience of pain. Because I have been hurt, and because I believe that you also are human, I imagine the suffering you feel when you are in pain. If I am guilty of causing that pain, the awareness that I have brought about something that I myself deem evil causes me to experience regret and shame. And because I have known joy, I'm able to recognize happiness in you. If I have contributed to your happiness, that knowledge makes me happy, too. Here reason and emotion are working together to create the power of empathy, and empathy is what makes conscience possible. Goodness does not come from the gods, it is a virtue arising from the power of human moral reasoning.

Omniscience: We are called *Homo Sapiens Sapiens,* the Wise Ones, because the modern human brain is unique among animals. Our intelligence is unparalleled, as the arts and sciences, language and mathematics bear witness. Humans are inquisitive and creative, always learning, remembering synthesizing and plotting the future. We do not know everything, but together we already have or can learn and share all the information we need to meet any challenge.

Omnipotence: We are bound by the laws of nature, but able to work within them to protect our fragile planet in the face of overpopulation and climate change. We have at our disposal all the resources of the earth to move mountains, propel ourselves into space, or blow ourselves to smithereens. But it is not only physical power that I ascribed to god, but also the power to move hearts and minds. I find myself called to choose between the use of force and coercion, or the powers of reason and love, in seeking the cooperation of others. All of these powers belong to all of us, for good or ill.

Omnipresence: Although the internet, television, and cell phones seem to bring all the world together, actually, in some ways we are farther apart than ever before. When we isolate ourselves in private, on-screen worlds, sometimes even when seated at the same table, we deny the other our life-affirming attention. We do well to remember that infants don't survive in the absence of touch, and that our need for the nearness of others continues throughout life. When we acknowledge that there is no god to be there for everyone in every moment, then we see that it is up to us to be there for each other.

•

Love, Righteousness, Omniscience, Omnipotence, and Omnipresence are the main qualities of the god I worshiped. They represent important powers that I want to reclaim and grow into. In believing that god was the source of these powers, I have spent most of my life with a diminished view of what it means to be human. I am now humbled and elevated at the same time to know that it is I who bless, I who create and sustain, and I who remember.

I hope that you will take some time to examine your own beliefs about what makes a god a god, and how those characteristics are reflections of what is most deeply and truly you.

•

Chapter Four: Establishing the Sanctuary

As you begin to see the holiness of your life, you may find that you want a special place where you can calm your thoughts and emotions in order to be nourished by the power of your inner spirit. It may seem odd at first to think of creating something like a sanctuary and altar in your home. You may not feel the need for them, or even the right to have them. Sanctuaries and altars are thought of as places to worship a god. And since the communion you are seeking is with your own spirit, and you certainly don't intend to start worshiping yourself, what is the purpose of establishing a place to retreat in private?

It has been my experience that the needs of the spirit are very simple: only a little bit of time, and my full attention. A place in which you can be alone, perhaps with a focal point to center on and maybe some soft instrumental music, will help to quiet your thoughts and emotions and draw you into that attitude of full attention to the spirit.

Call it meditation, mindful breathing or centering, all that is really involved in creating a holy moment in your sanctuary is being quiet, inside and out. And sometimes that's hard to do. The time you give yourself to retreat in your sanctuary is time that you are not devoting to the needs of others, to work, children, chores, art, exercise, and a hundred other things. Your commitment of time and attention may also entail a sacrifice on the part of others in your household as they agree not to disturb you. The physical benefits of meditation, even beyond the opening of spirit, are well-documented, and I do hope you will give sanctuary-keeping a fair trial before deciding whether the inconvenience outweighs the benefits.

When you decide to take time for spirit, whether or not you are able to enter your physical sanctuary, one of the simplest ways to center down into your silence and deep attention is by observing your breathing. Many teachers have offered good advice on how to breathe mindfully. You may find that if you are withdrawing during a time of stress, you won't be able to just jump into meditation. First you will need to calm your breathing and become centered, meaning that you will focus your thoughts and emotions together on something neutral, something that does not require analysis or tug at your heartstrings. A good choice is your breathing, your footsteps, the drip of water, your feet cycling on the pedals, or anything simple enough that you can tune it out along with everything else, shut down, and go within.

For a retreat in your sanctuary, sit erect on a chair or floor cushion. If you lie down you may fall asleep. If you feel agitated at first, remember that, as the moment lengthens, your muscles will relax more and more. Begin with a deep cleansing breath. Then draw in a longer, slower breath, expanding both belly and lungs, counting to seven as you fill up with fresh air nearly to bursting. When you reach maximum fullness, hold the breath as you count to five. Then, through pursed lips, allow the breath to escape to a count of seven. Hold the exhale for a count of five. Repeat. Do all of this three times. Then sit quietly, breathing slowly and regularly, noticing the rise and fall of your chest.

Notice if there are any tense places in your body. Imagine focusing the healing power of your own warm circulation on those spots, letting them relax more and more. Gradually you will lose track of your thoughts and emotions as you become attuned only to your breathing. Occasionally thoughts will enter, but let them drift away. There's plenty of time for that later. This holy moment is your very own.

It has been my experience that when my thoughts are quiet and I am focused on something I have no particular emotion about, such as breathing or walking, then my spirit is freed to speak. The challenge then is simply to listen. The spirit does not speak in words, but its inspiring energy might flow so fast that it stirs insights and revelations in you so rapidly that you can hardly catch it all, or so slowly that it seems no more than a pulsing silence. Whatever your experience feels like, just waiting in silence nourishes, renews and strengthens the body, mind and heart in ways that will stay with you.

•

Within your sanctuary you may want to have an altar. It can be as simple as a single candle or a rock on a piece of fabric. It might be something elaborate with representations of many things that are meaningful to you. It can be hard at first to give yourself permission to do this. The teachings of your former religion may be cautioning you against claiming the truth of your own witness. Especially if you are a woman, centuries of male control over the altars and trappings of religion may have made you reluctant to establish an altar in your own home. As I have made my way through this new territory of atheism, I have drawn encouragement from many sources, including "The Women's Well," where the founders write:

> *"In working with altars, we were tapping into something very deep in all of us.... When we talked about it together we realized that many of us already had sacred corners in our homes. We had places where, without thinking much about it or calling it anything special, we had put objects of beauty around, natural objects like stones or feathers, or something else that felt sacred to us. If someone who didn't understand their significance left a coffee cup or a notebook there, it would bother us and we would remove it. We also realized that many of us had been making centerpieces on our dinner tables for years, without considering that this too was altar making. Some of the women remembered that their mothers did this, too, as they set the table each night. We*

> *saw that the impulse to make altars was deep in the unconscious of women, and that in many ways we were reclaiming this ability, as we were reclaiming so much of ourselves that had been lost. As we made these sacred ways conscious, we could use them more intentionally in our own lives.... Altar making and the transforming of physical space into sacred space was one of the many strengths of women that had been buried...."*

"The Women's Well" at www.womenswell.org

Emboldened by their words, I arranged a small space to be a kind of sanctuary for myself, and in it I created an altar on the top of my drop-front desk. As I chose that corner of the guest room I had no clear idea of what the finished setting would look like, but I did realize how lucky I was to have that extra space in my house and that drop-front desk as its focal point. If places where you can be alone are hard to come by, then you might think also in terms of time. Is there some regular time when a certain area is not used, or could be closed off? It may be that you will have to negotiate with others to get time and a place to be alone. It might be that you won't be able to have a private space. If so, think about creating a small, portable altar in a box.

It's a delightful challenge to name the things that are holy to you, and that you want to represent on your altar. What do you value most in life? Can you find or make objects that represent those core values, and are small enough to place on your altar? This is especially challenging if you are making a box altar. But the labor is worthwhile and will bear spiritual fruit. The things I brought into my sanctuary are objects that I hoped would resonate with my spirit, call me deep into myself, and invite me to momentarily let go of the world of family and work. Each one represents some aspect of my life that is important to me.

I placed a pottery vase on my desk, holding a few stems of dried eucalyptus. I placed a candle beside the vase. On the wall facing me above the desk I hung a framed lithograph of a young face, done, apparently in haste, by Picasso. My native American flute and a drum I made from a gourd hang nearby. Inside the desk I put my journal and writing materials.

I studied these artifacts and believed I had found the first few of my sacred symbols. The eucalyptus leaves and the young face symbolized life and living things. The fire represented spirit, the spark of life itself. The flute and drum represented the wordless truths of the spirit's wisdom. It was a good beginning.

I have long thought that Scandinavian people are superior to Americans in many ways, and the latest example may be found in the book *The Gentle Art of Swedish Death Cleaning* by Margareta Magnusson. This method of down-sizing courageously faces the fact that many of us will approach the end of life packed to the gills with worldly belongings our children and grandchildren probably won't want. Older Swedes are purging their households of duplicates and excesses, and holding family meetings to discuss what's worth passing on and what's not. It is a win-win solution. The cleaner ends up surrounded by the best of the best, and the family will not have to deal with a mess later on.

In the process of decluttering, filling bags for the thrift store, planning a sale, or recycling papers, you may come across things that stop you in your tracks and beg you to look at them, hold them in your hands, and remember their story. These things may carry deep meaning for you as symbols of the life of your spirit. It's possible they might belong on your altar.

When I was trying to pare down the contents of a box of decorative items I keep in the bottom of the dining room hutch, I found the usual things. What to do with the rooster and hen that always sat on the round shelves in my mother's kitchen, or the one thing I have from Denny's mother: a little glued-together Carter's ink bottle in the shape of a man with a top hat. Hard decisions.

But what about these? There were the stone tools I had found lying in the grass as I strolled around the lake on one of our summer vacations long ago. I say they are tools but I don't know what they might have been used for. The first is shaped something like a spear point, but is not flattened or sharpened on any edge. It's about five inches long. One end has been shaped somewhat into a rounded wedge, the other end into a dull point. It is perfectly hand-sized and has a wonderful heavy weight to it. I don't know what it is.

The second tool is about the size and shape of an open hand. It is flat, being perhaps one half inch think around the edges, and an inch thick at the middle. In the thickest part of the center a depression has been ground out, like the navel in a belly. The tip of my thumb fits perfectly into the hollow, but I have no idea what this might have been made for. Is it a small mortar and if I had looked further might I have found its tiny pestle? I know it's not a fire-starter to be used with a bow drill because those would be made of something that will burn. It's clearly meant to hold something small. Did it stabilize one leg of a tripod that held a pot over a fire?

These mysterious tools had been in that box ever since I found them. I brought them out and placed them on my desk altar next to the candle. And seeing them there I felt a deep sense of their rightness. But I saw also that their presence challenged the meaning I had previously assigned to the other objects: the clay pot of eucalyptus seemed now to speak more of death than life, the candle now stood out as the spark of life and love, the drawing and the drum and the flute spoke of the pleasures of play and artistic expression, as the stone tools spoke of everyday's labor and toil. These four symbols seemed to work together to form a whole: life and love, toil, art and play, death. And these are bound together by a fifth element, which is in me, in my spirit. I liked how this made me feel.

Symbols are designed by humans to represent to our senses what is known to our spirit. In establishing your own symbols, you may wish to honor the sacred objects of an existing religious tradition, or gather a few objects that have personal history for you, or even make something that represents a deeply held truth or value. The process may involve recognizing the inherent holiness of an everyday object. In that case you will take it upon yourself to declare it holy, setting it aside from a common to a sacred purpose.

Over time, some symbols may lose their power for you and others may emerge as new understandings arise. I encourage you to approach the quest for your own sacred symbols from two different angles. The first is to simply ask yourself to name your highest values. Considering the fact that you have lived the life you've lived, and that you are exactly who and where you are, bring to your awareness whatever it is about your journey that seems most profoundly true and lasting. Do you have, or can you find or make, objects that represent those qualities or values? If so, bring them into your sanctuary. If they are small enough to fit on your altar, place them there.

Another way to discover your symbols is to engage in the work of pruning and weeding your possessions. As I discovered when I came across the long forgotten stone tools, the process of tossing, recycling, selling and giving stuff away may bring you face to face with something you absolutely cannot part with. What is it? Do you know why it is so important to you? What does it represent? This might be one of your sacred objects. Bring it to your sanctuary and see if it does, or does not, bring you into closer communion with your spirit.

The altar you have prepared should not distract you from the work of seeking spirit within, but rather should consist of the merest shadows of what you believe to be true and lasting. It is probably not best to include photos and mementos of people you're likely to start thinking about, nor items that will remind you of family, work, hobbies, or major responsibilities. Anything that will pull you into a mental conversation or is likely to stir up strong emotions should probably be avoided if you are seeking silent commune with your spirit. On the other hand, if you are doing grief work, by all means set aside a special time to surround yourself with everything that brings the loved one close. Settle in and allow the process to unfold with all your heart and mind and spirit.

The altar is merely a focal point, a small distraction to help you pull away from tumbling thoughts and feelings. Let it be a calming arrangement of simple things.

The use of a focal point to distract and center the mind is perhaps nowhere better used than in the Lamaze method of preparation for childbirth. We mothers-to-be were asked to bring something to look at, anything from a piece of paper to a small stuffed animal, anything that could be taped to the wall, tied to the bed, or propped up where we could see it during labor. In class we lay on the floor and gazed at our focal point. We were asked to make a tight fist with one hand while engaging in a progressive whole-body relaxation exercise. Our partner-coach crawled around our body checking neck muscles, wrists, knees and ankles to make sure they could be moved freely without any sign of tension, coming back frequently to be sure the fist was still rigid. As I gazed at my focal point, my vision blurred. A kind of soft trance-like state set in. Our instructor softly paced the room, reminding us in a quiet voice that our clenched fist was like the contracted uterus, and that our ability to maintain relaxation during a contraction would allow the baby to pass through without unnecessary resistance, thus causing less pain.

The focal point, of course, is nothing. Like any good symbol it is merely a finger pointing to something greater than itself. So it is with the sacred space, the altar within it, and the little objects on the altar. All of these are mere stand-ins for the truth that is within you.

The making of gods and symbols is a deep mystery. When language fails we turn to silence, or to the wordless approximation of symbols. From the dawn of consciousness humans have sought to understand what's really going on here: am I really the center of the universe, which is how it feels? Is that the meaning of the mandalas and labyrinths that are found in nearly every culture? When I wake up everything appears in its fullness, when I close my eyes it goes away, and when I feel a thing I am alone in my experience. Questions arise, if not from within myself then from the child who looks up and asks, "Why did that happen? Who am I? What is that? Where are we?" Unable to answer our own questions or those of the children, we wonder if all of this might be planned and ordered by One we cannot see, and if it all makes sense to that One in a way we cannot yet understand.

I have come to the conclusion that I am that One: it's in me that all of these things are ordered and come together in a way that makes sense to me. And allowing that to be true for me requires that I also allow the very same for you. You are the center of the universe of your own experience, just as I am the center of mine. It is in you, and you alone, that the things you discover come together in a way that makes sense to you. The universe appears when you open your eyes and disappears when you close them. Fire means something to you that I cannot fathom, as does art, and death, and family.

And so now, when I am in a crowd, I look around at the different faces that are not my face, each one the center if its own universe, each one capable of snuffing out my existence by closing its eyes, and I am frightened to be in the presence of so many gods.

•

Today I'm writing at my small desk in the guest room sanctuary of my house. The door is closed and soft music is playing quietly from a cd player on the dresser behind me. A white candle burns in front of me on the desktop altar, just below the lithographed portrait of "Roby" by Pablo Picasso. The boy's dear and tranquil face is merely suggested by a few quickly and expertly drawn lines. In his simple gaze I find a trace of everyone I love, even, at times, of myself.

In this room I am utterly alone, with things that inspire me. There are no reminders of my husband, my children, or my grandchildren. There are no toys or decorator items. The rest of my house is devoted to hobbies and cooking and the sometimes jolly, sometimes stressful, doings of family. But not here. With Roby above me and a flat metal sea turtle sculpture above the headboard, I'm alone with mere symbols of life and its eternal mystery.

I didn't know this convergence was possible in my life until it happened. I didn't know I could have all of this, and maybe it wasn't even possible until now. Or maybe I was not fully ready until now to receive this gift, this entry, this opening into a new way and truth and life.

The ancient Greeks spoke of time in two ways: chronos, referring to the simple passage of time, and chairos, referring to the perfection of a moment in the fullness of time. Things may be coming together for you in such a way that you feel heavy with ripening. Whether you realize it or not, something new may be ready to emerge. Look around. Look within. It's possible that you have everything you need to claim a sacred space and live into holy moments. You have suffered losses and rejoiced in receiving. You've learned much and rejected more. You have hurt and you have been hurt. You have loved and been loved. It may be that each of us is only able to sit in communion with our spirit on the foundation of these fortunes. Even though this chairos moment is not the fruit of your labor alone, it is still uniquely yours.

•

As you consider creating your own sanctuary, remember that the physical space you bless is an outward expression of the sanctuary that is always already within you. The physical sanctuary exists to serve the spiritual one. This also means that wherever you may be, your spiritual sanctuary is always there to receive and restore you.

But having said that, I am writing this because I've found that I need this physical sanctuary, this place of safety and peace, surrounded by objects that call my spirit to expand. Much as the sanctuary at church used to invoke a sense of wonder, I now find that this place opens me up to my spirit in a whole new way.

Your sanctuary, however small it may be, will over time come to trigger a response in you that feels like peace, comingled with expectation, and tinged with awe. As you become accustomed to the joy of finding yourself there in this sacred place that reflects back to you what is most real in your life, it will become easier and easier to relax and slip your mind, your heart and your breathing into a meditative state, and set your spirit free.

Whether long or short, the time you take for spirit creates a structure through which its transforming power more easily enters. Of course, spiritual gifts cannot be scheduled to arrive on demand. But when time for silence and meditation is taken, and arrangements are made to ensure your comfort and full attention, those holy moments can bear spiritual fruit.

In creating your sanctuary, try to find a place where you can be alone whenever you want to. Clean and arrange it to minimize distractions. Consecrate the space, and give it your blessing. Perhaps you might say something like this:

> *"Today I bless this place and declare it holy:*
> *it shall be a welcoming home for my spirit.*
> *With joy I set this place, and all that is in it aside*
> *from a common to a sacred purpose.*
> *I commit myself to entering with an open heart,*
> *willing to listen and learn.*
> *From this day forward, the time I spend here is holy."*

Perhaps you will want to frame your time in the sanctuary with an opening and closing phrase or a gesture. I often whisper to myself, "Be here now." Sometimes I light the candle. I also have a small bell. Consider playing soft music, anointing your wrists with fragrant oil, or lighting incense if it feels right for you.

Silence is the greatest tool for enlightenment. A silent room will allow you to enter the stillness of your soul and listen there for whatever truth is rising. I often note similarities between prayer and the spiritual questing I engage in in my sanctuary. Prayer and meditation are alike in that they often involve a protracted period of listening for an unspoken answer to a silent question.

Prayer shapes the heart and will of the one praying. In a similar way, meditation lifts thought and emotion into the realm of spirit, where the power of human transformation resides. The difference between the two is that, while the one who prays looks outward, the one who meditates looks within. It may be that there is a kind of unnatural dependency in prayer that is overcome in affirming one's own holiness and wisdom.

The silence of mindful meditation is a silence unlike any other. When I focus on my breathing I am tuning out the rest of who I am and what I know. As I let my breath flow in and out naturally I am suspending all judgement. There is no thought, and no emotion: only my silent awareness of my breath, and nothing else. And what rises to fill that void is spirit.

The first paradox of mindful meditation is that, while it serves to ground me in the present moment, and intently focuses me on my breathing, loosening my panicky grip on everything else, it's then, in that moment of intense focus, that my spirit is most free to emerge and rise into my awareness. The secret seems to be that I have no judgement about my breath. It just comes and goes, in and out, and although I know I can't live without it, I have no conscious emotional attachment to it. So, in mindful attention to my breathing I have shut down not only my thoughts but also my emotions. That opens the gap through which spirit rises.

Any activity can become a mindful practice. Mindfulness begins with your intention to be completely present to an experience, a place, an object, or a simple activity. In mindful experiencing your intention is always to honor the moment by noticing details, taking in information with all of your senses. The hard part, but the fruitful part which opens the spiritual gap, lies in being fully present to the moment without placing a value judgement on its content, but instead honoring the experience itself as sacred, and the time you spend with it as holy.

The second paradox of *mindfulness* is that it involves a shift from one kind of *mindlessness* to another. We go through much of life on mindless autopilot, moving from one thing to the next without really living any of them, feeling alternately resentful, remorseful, anxious or hopeful in the monotony of it all. But the mindlessness that happens in mindful focus is a paradoxical forgetting of self, a kind of mental and emotional emptiness that allows spirit to rise and expand. The stilling of the heart and focusing of the mind on a simple activity opens the gap for spirit to come to your awareness. You may find it when you focus on listening to your breath, or mowing the lawn, walking, or doing laundry. Anything can be done mindfully and so become an occasion for spiritual awakening.

•

At the conclusion of your time in the sanctuary, signal your gratitude and your readiness to return to the ordinary business of life. You might take a deep breath or give a happy clap, extinguish the candle, or ring the bell. I often whisper, "Thank you," and make a drawing-in gesture with my hands, bringing them to lay over my heart as a way of sealing what I have received. Do whatever signals to you that this special time has ended for now, and that it's time to go. Take with you fresh energy, and the assurance that your sanctuary is always there, waiting for you in this room, and in the stillness of your heart wherever you may be.

Chapter Five: The Mystery of Spirit

No one knows what spirit is. Whatever spirit may be, it is not the words of thought, nor the thrills and chills of emotion. The human spirit seems to be a third faculty that we possess, beyond thought and emotion. I have asked myself whether spirit might be the physical spark that animates the raw materials from which we are made, and whether that spark might be drawn from the fire power of the universe itself. I wonder if our spirit is the mere awareness of being, or the mark of sentient existence, or the pressure of the infinite. No one knows. We only know that when we silence the mind and the heart, there remains a vital, pulsing presence.

German existential philosopher Martin Heidegger does not speak directly of the human spirit, but he describes the human condition as one in which we find ourselves "thrown" here into this life, as though washed up on a shore. We don't know where we came from, how we got here, or why we are here. We know only that we exist and that our time here is limited. That may not seem like much, but Heidegger insists that it is the knowledge that we are finite and how we cope with the anxiety this produces, that makes us authentically human.

Heidegger names this poor, washed-up human being "Dasein," the One Who Is. As Dasein, I know I will die and that everything I see and touch is temporary. I have the ability to contemplate the nothingness from which I came and to which I will return. This knowledge causes me to live in existential dread. Heidegger maintains that when Dasein is distracted from the truth of his or her finitude by the busy-ness of doing, then Dasein is living inauthentically. The authenticity of the human being lies in his or her acceptance of the weight of dread, and in being there for others while knowingly and courageously living toward death and nothingness. This heady teaching reminds me of the more down-to-earth words of Mark Twain, who wrote, "Courage is resistance to fear, mastery of fear, not absence of fear."

I wonder if in meditation, as we let go of all thoughts and feelings in order to more fully experience our own spiritual vitality, we are somehow reconnecting with our existential thrown-ness, our helplessness, and our authentic need for others.

Plato imagined that all of the human virtues and powers exist as ideal forms in an ideal realm somewhere outside of us. It is heartening to think of the quality of perfect generosity, for example, as actually existing somewhere as a pure ideal, setting a goal for us and calling us to live more generous lives, leading us toward the fulfillment of our highest potential. In my view, Plato was correct in his belief that pure forms of the human virtues and powers exist, but I believe that he erred in projecting these ideals outside of the human spirit. The ideal forms of all that is highest and best do exist, but within us, not outside of us. They are part of who and what we are born to be. They urge us to strive toward ever higher forms of goodness, and they tweak our conscience when we turn away from them.

Plato's error, in placing human goodness in another realm outside of our life as we live it, is what lead to the idea of the immortal soul. The belief that we exist in two parts, a physical body and a spiritual soul, known as dualism, flourished in ancient Greece and was carried by the teachings of Paul into the Jewish sect who first followed Jesus of Nazareth. That group of early Jewish followers would have viewed the human body and spirit as indistinguishable and inseparable from one another. But when Paul's Greek dualistic thinking later reshaped the gospel to appeal to the minds of Greek converts, it almost entirely replaced the Hebrew notion of the earthbound spirit with the dualistic idea of eternal life. A vestige of the original Hebrew belief can be seen in the doctrine of the bodily resurrection. But in the end it is Plato whom we must credit for the persistent modern belief that the human spirit has an eternal life of its own, independent of the body.

Does the human spirit reside in the brain the way thoughts take place in the prefrontal cortex, and emotions are centered in the amygdala? Is spirit independent of the body? Or is spirit somehow suffused through the body as its life force? While I maintain that the human spirit undeniably exists, and that it is neither thought nor emotion, I must also admit that it would not be possible to identify any one area of the brain as its location. I must ask, then, in suggesting that there is a distinction between the body and the body's life force or spirit, am I embracing a kind of dualism? And if so, does this require crossing the line into supernaturalism?

I do believe that spirit is energy and the body is matter. I believe that spirit is the animating force of the body, and therefore spirit is not quite identical with the body. However, the human spirit is dependent on the body as the place where it expresses itself as life. And so it doesn't seem to me that this low grade kind of dualism necessitates the position of a supernatural spiritual realm. It only suggests to me that energy is more that just the physical force that powers the laws of nature: it is also the source and destiny of my life. I believe that because that universal energy is a unitary wholeness, it holds all spirits together.

But as humans, we experience life as individual spirits isolated from one another. I wonder if the attraction between human beings, which drives us to each other and inclines us to work toward common goals, to share and to help and protect each other and build societies, I wonder if that spiritual drive represents the drive of the energy of the universe to regather its scattered sparks. If so, then what we call love no longer seems like a romantic notion, but more like an elemental force.

And is the human spirit somehow folded into the Gaia? According to this theory, the human spirit is part of a cooperative energy that drives every living thing on earth to work together toward the preservation of the conditions that make life on earth possible. Believers view our efforts to establish off-world colonies as evidence that we are driven to do anything, to use all of our powers and resources, to ensure the continuation of life.

Spirit is not thought, but it expresses itself in philosophy and religion and mathematics and art. Spirit is not emotion, but it expresses itself in love and anxiety and grief and joy. Whether it is because all human spirits partake of one great energy which lives in each of us and is seeking its own wholeness, or because we can see that other humans are like us and we empathize with their condition and so want to help them, whatever the case, the human spirit is undeniably drawn to other spirits.

•

In my small sanctuary I am alone with my own spirit. I am comforted to withdraw into my center and find my spirit always there, within me, shining and still. What I have begun to see about this mysterious spirit that dwells within and through me, and which may participate in an infinite spirit, and which longs for connection with other spirits, is that it seems to have the shocking ability to shed me like a skin and emerge to stand alone in the world. This has happened to me so rarely that it's hard to describe, and so all I can do is give a few examples. In those moments, I am present more as observer than actor.

•

The first time my spirit seemed to kick me out of the way to enter the world I was twenty-two years old, still grieving the death of my bother, and had just learned that I was pregnant with our first child. Back in those days there were no at-home pregnancy test kits. The call from the doctor came to me at work. I was still living in a fog of grief and this news was a strong wind that cleared the air. I was overjoyed at the news that a baby was going to come home to us and fill my arms and soothe my heart. Somehow I knew this child would be a girl (and she was). As I rode the elevated train home through downtown Chicago, I set my purse on the seat between my coat and the window. Stopped at a station, I looked down at my purse and imagined a small blond head bent intently over it, exploring its contents with little fingers, pulling out this and that to show me. I softened inwardly and outwardly. My muscles went slack, my heart went out to her, my eyes filled with tears and I smiled with the deepest joy I had ever known. I gazed over her head out the window and there, gazing back at me, was a man at a sewing machine, not more than fifteen feet away. He was behind the window of a second story tailor's shop, but the reflections vanished and the distance between us shrank to nothing as our eyes locked into each other. He began to rise from his seat. He leaned over the machine toward me until he could lean no farther. A strange expression transformed his face as though he were seeing something he didn't understand but wanted to touch. I felt his intense presence in my mind, but the train jerked forward and we moved on. I pondered his gaze, I saw his heart: I believed he had not seen me, but what Catholics see in Mary.

•

The second time my spirit broke through was when our second daughter was a little over a year old. The transformation I had experienced at the prospect of motherhood had held. The depression and grief had retreated and my two girls were the center of my life, my salvation, my pride and joy. As I lay my baby in her crib one night after nursing her full and reading her to sleep, I stood a moment in the dim light just gazing at her soft face and the little lump she formed under her yellow blanket. As I stood I sensed a nudge from within and, although it sounds strange even to me as I recall it, it seemed that a spiritual power was inviting me to close myself off from the moment so that this spirit might see my baby through human eyes. I was a jealously protective mother and I was reluctant to give up even a little of that tender moment, but I knew there would be more moments like this, and besides it was already happening -- and then it was over, and my baby was my own again.

•

My third, fourth and fifth experiences of spirit came within weeks of each other. The girls were in their late teens and with their busy lives they needed me less. I found myself with time to look inward and found that there was still considerable emotional pain there. I located a compassionate counselor who helped me see that in raising the girls I had left unfinished the grief work I had begun so long ago. I had closed myself off from many unresolved issues with my parents and sister regarding my brother's death. And so the work began. During one of our first sessions I tearfully confided that I wanted nothing more than to see him just one more time.

That night, after my husband had gone to sleep, I was sitting up in bed doing a crossword puzzle. I felt the urge to go downstairs. In my nightgown I tiptoed across the landing and down the dark stairwell. As I entered the living room everything was as bright as day. Sunlight was pouring in through the bay windows, and in front of them, in one of our wing chairs, sat my beloved brother. But he was not himself. He was translucent from head to toe, glowing with pale shimmering colors and pulsating light. Then he rose up out of the chair and began to walk toward me where I stood frozen in the doorway. As he approached the glowing colors of his body shifted through a spectrum of soft light, pink, blue, lavender, gold and pure, glowing white. And he was laughing.

His laughter was not the kind of laugh that comes from jokes, but the kind that comes from joy. He was overflowing with joy and yet so very still, he was speaking and yet silent, he was clearly recognizable and yet so very strange. I loved him and he loved me. He reassured me that he was more than okay and that I should not be sad about him any more. Joy filled my heart.

When I woke in the morning I remembered everything and wrote it all down in my journal, ready to share with my counselor.

... At that time, my sister was also living in Chicago. She was and still is a great believer in spirit, and she came over the next day to help me think this through. As we spoke of our brother and what he had meant to us and what had happened long ago and what had happened to me in recent days, I put on a recording of Brahms' German Requiem, a piece of music full of history and emotion for both of us. As we allowed our feelings to be enriched by the soaring chorus and orchestra we agreed that it was indeed possible that he had come to me in spirit because my spirit had called out to his in need. It seemed also that his spirit had met my need with an answer so satisfying and truthful that it had moved me into new territory, where healing could begin. As the strains of "How Lovely is Thy Dwelling Place" began, I climbed into my sister's lap and somehow felt that our brother's spirit was there with us, but slipping away. I felt it pulling upward like silk through my fingers. I reached as high as I could, and then he was gone, and I fell limp to the floor, sobbing in gratitude.

... But as it turned out he wasn't completely gone. I would find him one more time, and again it would involve the elevated trains of Chicago. I was then attending classes at the downtown campus of DePaul University, and rode the Lake Avenue el both ways. One afternoon, not long after my sister's visit, I got on board and took a seat next to a window on the right, facing forward. There were few others in the car, and I rested my head against the glass, gazing at the platform across the tracks. A black man stood there all alone, looking at me. As the train inched forward, the man raised his right hand and pressed it to his lips. As the train began to click along, he held the kiss out to me on his open hand. I turned in my seat to look more fully at him, and he smiled as he followed me, turning his body and stretching out his arm as far as he could. I knew this was my brother's final farewell to me as I slipped away from him, like silk pulled through his fingers.

•

I walked alone on a small, thickly wooded island in the middle of a rushing river in Wisconsin. Coffee-colored water churned noisily downhill on both sides of the island, toward a steep precipice over which it threw itself, causing a tremendous uproar in the pool below. The foaming water calmed itself as it flowed away through a level canyon.

The forest was old growth, having a canopy so dense, and a carpet of needles so thick, that nothing else grew there. Walking among the towering pines, it seemed to me that the columns and vaulted roofs of Greek temples were designed to recreate just this sense of timelessness, wonder and peace.

As I stood in a small clearing, the pounding of the river against the bedrock under my feet vibrated relentlessly. The vibrations rose up through the soles of my shoes and traveled up my spine. The sound filled my ears. The sun beat hot on my head. It seemed that I was absorbing energy from above, from below, and from the dark trunks all around me. I felt that I was reborn, and that anything was possible for me.

Wondering if I had actually been transfigured, I dug into my pack for my camera, looked squarely into the lens, and snapped the shutter (this was before cell phones and selfies). But when the prints came back a few weeks later I was disappointed to see an odd smile, but nothing out of the ordinary in my features.

•

When I was visiting in the desert southwest, my dear friend took me to a hot spring on the banks of the Rio Grande. We stripped to our bathing suits and stepped down into the steaming water. The river rushed by on the other side of a natural rock barrier, so close that I could reach out my arm and trail my fingers in its cold water. The sun shone on our hair as we gazed across the shining surface of the water at each other, sharing the love that abides between longtime friends who are separated by great distance. Time passed, and the heat of the water became too much. As we lazily considered the thought of standing up into the cold air and returning to the real world, a bird flew down and perched on the rocks two or three feet away. It began to sing. It's melody filled the canyon as it sang on and on. We listened, entranced and still. Then as quickly as she had come the bird took flight, dropping a solitary feather. It drifted slowly down and settled on the water delicately just in front of my face.

I kept the feather for a long time. Like Dumbo, I didn't realize that I didn't really need it.

Chapter Six: Secular Morality

The urge to seek the company of others and live in communities is a basic biological drive. All living things feel it and are drawn to their own kind. Even in my worst moments, when I'm so frustrated that "hermit" and "recluse" seem like good lifestyle choices, I eventually come to my senses and am glad for the human connections I have. Even though we do need some time alone, maybe more than we realize, we can't live fully if we are completely cut off from other humans.

Sometimes I have to remind myself that the profound and lasting moral teachings of the world's great religions were written entirely by humans. If there was a god who inspired any of them, that god, too, was created by humans. The fact that religious teachings often become the pillars of great societies does not credit the imaginary gods who are said to be revealed in them, but rather stand as tribute to the human moral thinkers, poets and philosophers who drafted them. The Upanishads, the Koran, the Bible owe nothing to supernatural influence of any sort. They are entirely and beautifully human in origin, and are outstanding examples of the synthesis of the human mind, heart and spirit.

Anthropologists and sociologists have done a great service in helping us to see the human, as opposed to divine, origins of laws, ethical behavior, community-building and moral reasoning. In studying patterns of communal living among both humans and animals, scientists have pointed out that certain kinds of unselfish behavior toward others actually increase our own chances of survival. They have found that it can be in our best interest as individuals to cooperate with others and help them when they are in need, with the mutual understanding that they will return the favor when we are in need. Quite apart from any rulings from on high to love our neighbor, we see with our own eyes, feel in our heart, and know by spirit-to-spirit contact with others that our personal survival may depend on each of us doing what we can to ensure the survival of the whole group.

In working toward a master's in continental philosophy, I titled my thesis "Empathy and Ethics." I focused on the work of two phenomenologists in particular, Edmund Husserl and his student Edith Stein. Between them we are given to understand that, even though all human experience is subjective, it is still possible to understand the thoughts and emotions of another human being. That capacity is called empathy, and it is the foundation on which relationships of all kinds are built.

To roughly summarize their work, empathic understanding is actually a function of psychological projection. In other words, in empathizing with you, I understand what you are probably thinking or feeling because I can remember what I felt like when I was in the situation you are in. I project my own subjective responses onto you in the belief that you are a subject, too, just as I am. And if we are alike in that essential way, then I can safely assume that your response to the conditions you're facing will be similar to my own response. I imagine, without feeling your pain, that you are feeling pain when I see that you have been hurt. Likewise, when I see you eat chocolate, I remember that pleasure, and I can imagine your pleasure.

The ability to imagine what others are experiencing by projecting our own experience onto them generally develops when children are around seven years old. An amusing test involves showing a child a piece of cardboard which is black on one side and white on the other. The child holds it, examines it, turns it over and over. When the adult holds the card up with the black side facing the child and asks, "What do you see?" the child will correctly answer, "Black." But when asked, "What do I see?" a young child will again answer, "Black." But a child who has developed the ability to imagine and project the experience of others, that is, a child who is capable of empathic understanding, will answer, "White."

But how does empathy relate to love, which is neither a power of mind nor of heart, but rather is a force of spirit? Empathy itself is not love, but without empathy, we would not know how to express our love toward another person, nor guess what another person intends when acting upon us. Through empathy, humans are equipped to demonstrate love (or other emotions) to others by saying and doing things we know through our own experience will please or be helpful to the other. The tools of empathic understanding equip us also to live responsibly in community with complete strangers. This is possible because of our mutual understanding that each and every person we meet is a subjective human being like ourselves. The gift of empathy is the raw material that makes it possible to know right from wrong.

Empathy is the substance of conscience. Empathic understanding can be used just as easily for harm as it can be for good: if I want to hurt you, empathy reveals exactly how to do it most painfully. It is because I have the ability to know within myself when I have hurt you that I'm able to feel shame, and it's because I know what it feels like to be happy that I know when I have made you happy. I judge my actions as right or wrong based on empathic understanding of how my actions are likely to have affected you.

So if I want to be seen as a good person in my own eyes and in the eyes of others, if I hope to act in ways that benefit others rather than harm them, and if I no longer trust religious doctrine to shape my values, then is empathy the only resource I can turn to for judging my actions? Certainly empathy helps to guide me in interpersonal relationships, but because it is based on my own limited experience, I need more than that to help me discern right from wrong when faced with decisions that have more far-reaching effects. By what rules should I now live?

Where can I turn for moral guidance in my role as a member of society and the world?

The first place I want to turn is to the body whose sole purpose is the establishment of international peace and justice: the United Nations. *The United Nations Declaration of Human Rights* is based on the "Categorical Imperative" written in 1790 by German philosopher Immanuel Kant. Kant's Categorical Imperative states:

> *"Act only in accordance with that maxim through which you can at the same time will that it become a universal law."*

According to Kant's principle, ethical decision-making should be guided by considering what the world would be like if my action in this moment became a universal rule, so that in every situation like this my decision would be applied. My rule would thus affect everyone, and would potentially be enacted upon myself. This sounds like, and may have been inspired by, the "Golden Rule," which states that we ought to do to others what we would want them to do to us, and that we ought not do to others what we would not want done to ourselves.

The ideal of the morally responsible community is the foundation of the *UN Declaration of Human Rights*. Of the Thirty "Articles," or basic human rights, listed in the *Declaration*, I list here the first six:

> *Article 1 - All human beings are born free and equal in dignity and rights. They are endowed with reason and conscience and should act towards one another in a spirit of brotherhood.*
>
> *Article 2 - Everyone is entitled to all the rights and freedoms set forth in this Declaration, without distinction of any kind, such as race, color, sex, language, religion, political or other opinion, national or social origin, property, birth or other*

> status. Furthermore, no distinction shall be made on the basis of the political, jurisdictional or international status of the country or territory to which a person belongs, whether it be independent, trust, non-self-governing or under any other limitation of sovereignty.
>
> Article 3 - Everyone has the right to life, liberty and security of person.
>
> Article 4 - No one shall be held in slavery or servitude; slavery and the slave trade shall be prohibited in all their forms.
>
> Article 5 - Everyone has the right to recognition everywhere as a person before the law.
>
> Article 6 - No one shall be subjected to torture or to cruel, inhuman or degrading treatment or punishment.

The whole document is available from several sources, including www.un.org. It is a worthy model for anyone's personal credo of social responsibility.

•

Another thought-provoking and challenging resource is the legal systems of progressive nations. America was established under the rule of law. I found it interesting to follow the reasoning of the Supreme Court as they considered efforts in 2017 to limit the flow of immigrants into our country. Discussions between judges in the lower federal courts were streamed live on the internet and I listened with admiration as they weighed competing values. Even they needed to turn to one another for help in choosing the lesser of several evils, and the greater of several goods.

•

Another great resource for moral reasoning without religion is the vast library of Secular Humanist writing. As far as I know, no one has a bad thing to say about the Humanists, except for the few who hold that this moral philosophy is overly anthropocentric, placing the value of human life above the value of every other form of life, whether plant, animal, or extraterrestrial. Since my concern is primarily about how humans ought to relate to one another, I'm not very troubled by those concerns.

However, I must confess that the foundational statements of Humanism seemed at first to be somewhat hedonistic. There is a focus on living a joyful and enthusiastic life because this is the only life we have. I worried that Humanism might lack the moral courage to sacrifice self for the sake of others. But this was a superficial impression of the Humanist philosophy. At its heart, Secular Humanism is about a life of moral responsibility with concern for both self and others.

Edwin H. Wilson, an early proponent of Humanism, wrote:

> *The Humanist lives as if this world were all and enough. He is not otherworldly. He holds that the time spent on the contemplation of a possible afterlife is time wasted. He fears no hell and seeks no heaven, save that which he and others create on earth. He willingly accepts the world that exists on this side of the grave as the place for moral struggle and creative living. He seeks the life abundant for his neighbor as for himself.*

The following is taken from the *Secular Humanist Declaration*. The full text is available at the website of the Council for Secular Humanism:

> *"...ethics is an autonomous field of inquiry; ethical judgments can be formulated independently of revealed religion; human beings can cultivate practical reason*

and wisdom and, by their application, achieve lives of virtue and excellence."

The Declaration goes on to state that this philosophy is "opposed to absolutist morality," yet maintains that "objective standards may emerge, and ethical values and principles may be discovered, in the course of ethical deliberation."

The A*merican Humanist Association* states:

"Humanism is a progressive life-stance that, without theism or other supernatural beliefs, affirms our ability and responsibility to lead meaningful, ethical lives capable of adding to the greater good of humanity....we encourage, wherever possible, the growth of moral awareness, the capacity for free choice, and an understanding of the consequences thereof."

I was pleased to learn about Secular Humanism and have found great encouragement in its teachings.

•

And of course, for the late John Lennon, the moral life was not hard to imagine:

Imagine there's no heaven; It's easy if you try
No hell below us; Above us only sky
Imagine all the people living for today
Imagine there's no countries; It isn't hard to do
Nothing to kill or die for; And no religion too
Imagine all the people living life in peace
You may say I'm a dreamer; But I'm not the only one
I hope some day you'll join us
And the world will be as one.
Imagine no possessions; I wonder if you can
No need for greed or hunger; A brotherhood of man
Imagine all the people sharing all the world
You may say I'm a dreamer

But I'm not the only one
I hope some day you'll join us
And the world will be as one
                By John Winston Lennon/The Plastic Ono Band

•

I have loved the poem "Desiderata" since I was a teenager. These days it has become as holy to me as any scripture ever was. Line by line, the advice has stood the test of time and changing circumstance. I offer it below, broken into stanzas, with a daily intention offered as one possible way to understand each passage. Of course, there are countless ways to read the wisdom it contains.

Twenty-eight Days of *Desiderata*

Poem by Max Ehrmann, Copyright 1952
Reflections by Carol Maher

Day 1   ***Go placidly amid the noise and haste,***
> It can be a scary world out there. Today I intend to be mindful of the calm that resides in the deepest part of my soul.

Day 2   ***and remember what peace there may be in silence.***
> Today I intend to draw deeply from the reservoir of silence in my soul. In that still water is love for myself and for the world.

Day 3   ***As far as possible without surrender be on good terms with all persons.***
> Today I intend to honor the integrity of others as I honor my own. Their story is as true as mine. Their purpose is as real as mine.

Day 4 ***Speak your truth quietly and clearly;***
> Today I intend to be confident in my own truth. Confidence does not raise its voice, nor hide its gifts behind false modesty or a flood of words.

Day 5 ***Listen to others, even the dull and the ignorant, for they too have their story.***
> Today I intend, as far as I am able, to walk a mile in the moccasins of those whom I meet, or whom I am tempted to judge from afar.

Day 6 ***Avoid loud and aggressive persons, they are a vexation to the spirit.***
> Today I intend to be assertive rather than aggressive in my speech and actions, and mindful of my tone so that I do not offend.

Day 7 ***If you compare yourself with others you may become vain and bitter, for always there will be greater and lesser persons than yourself.***
> Today I intend to remember that I am enough, just as I am, and to honor each one I meet as my equal in value.

Day 8 ***Enjoy your achievements as well as your plans.***
> Today I intend to be proud of what I have accomplished, and I intend to be optimistic as I lay groundwork for the future.

Day 9 ***Keep interested in your own career, however humble; it is a real possession in the changing fortunes of time.***
> Today I intend to take pride in my work, for I have developed valuable knowledge and skills.

Day 10 ***Exercise caution in your business affairs for the world is full of trickery,***
> Today I intend to leave gullibility behind. I have seen enough to know that where there is an advantage to be taken, many will take it. I will avoid being taken. And I will not be the taker.

Day 11 ***But let this not blind you to what virtue there is,***
for many persons strive for high ideals,

>Today I intend to notice courageous people and to learn from their example. I intend to honor lovingkindness and honesty wherever I find it, and endeavor to grow toward these virtues.

Day 12 ***and everywhere life is full of heroism.***

>Today I intend to be a hero. If there is dissent, I will not press my case. If I have been injured, I will pardon. I will express my thanks to heroes wherever I find them.

Day 13 ***Be yourself.***

>Today I intend to speak truth in love to all I meet. I intend to avoid both judgement and flattery. I will not pretend to be wiser than I am, nor to know what I do not know. I will not be ashamed of my life, but will carry it with pride.

Day 14 ***Especially, do not feign affection.***

>Today I intend to be honest about my feelings, never fawning and promising when I mean something else, remembering that love is a spiritual power, not a ploy to be used for gain.

Day 15 ***Neither be cynical about love,***
for in the face of all aridity and disenchantment,
it is as perennial as the grass.

>Today I intend to freely give and receive love. I will not let disappointment keep me from loving, nor cause me to doubt another's love.

Day 16 ***Take kindly the counsel of the years,***

>Today I intend to listen carefully to my elders and allow them to help me see the past as context for the present and future.

Day 17 ***gracefully surrendering the things of youth.***
>Today I intend to welcome signs of aging as traces of the life I have lived, the loves I have known, the losses I have suffered, and the laughter that has tickled me from head to toe.

Day 18 ***Nurture inner strength to shield you in sudden misfortune.***
>Today I intend to honor the resolve that has seen me through many trials. I know that I can stand strong because I have done it before, and I am better equipped now than I have ever been.

Day 19 ***But do not distress yourself with dark imaginings, for many fears are born of fatigue and loneliness.***
>Today I intend to be clear about what threats are real and which are not. I will prepare myself to meet real challenges and dangers as I become aware of them. But I will not hide from life.

Day 20 ***Beyond a wholesome discipline, be gentle with yourself.***
>Today I intend to eat well, exercise, work hard, be kind to others and clean up my messes. Where I succeed in this, I will be glad. Where I fail, I will receive tomorrow as the gift of a chance to try again.

Day 21 ***You are a child of the universe,***
>I am made from the same elements that make up the stars and planets. The empty spaces between the atoms of my body are proportionate to the voids of our solar system. Today I intend to honor myself and others as made of star stuff.

Day 22 ***no less than the trees and the stars.***
>Today I intend to celebrate my place in nature. Every part of the earth is sacred. I'm glad to be alive, and I'm ready to learn all I can about where I am.

Day 23 ***You have a right to be here.***
>Today I intend to let go of false modesty. I am a strong person with modest gifts. I intend to give of myself, and welcome the gifts of others.

Day 24 ***And whether or not it is clear to you, the universe is no doubt unfolding as it should.***
>Today I intend to heed the advice of the Serenity Pledge, to "*accept what I cannot change, change what I can, and recognize the difference.*"

Day 25 ***Whatever your labors and aspirations, in the noisy confusion of life, keep peace with your soul.***
>Today I intend to take time to meditate. The silent sanctuary within me is a sacred place where I can retreat at any time to be restored.

Day 26 ***With all its sham, drudgery, and broken dreams, it is still a beautiful world.***
>Today I intend to affirm the inherent beauty of the world and the goodness of humankind, even in the midst of terrible news, exhausting labor, frustration and sorrow. There is beauty in me, and in each of us, and in the order of things.

Day 27 ***Be cheerful.***
>Today I intend to offer friendship and hope wherever I can. I intend to see my cup as half full rather than half empty.

Day 28 ***Strive to be happy.***
>Today I intend to celebrate what I have done and what I hope to do. I intend to celebrate the love I have for others and their love for me. I intend to be grateful for the time I have lived and for the time yet to come. I intend to embrace this holy day and live it to the fullest.

•

Even after religious belief fades, you may still miss the group you once belonged to. If your faith was strong and your religious life an active one, then you have lost more than just your faith: you have lost a community with whom you shared a worldview and a mission.

But embrace this new life as an opportunity to express the virtues of your soul in your own way. If you were in the habit of regular prayer, give yourself plenty of opportunity to meditate, allowing thoughts and emotions to sink away and your own dear spirit to rise and give your strength. Remember, there was never anyone there in prayer but you anyway. If you were in the habit of giving to your house of worship, give generously now to your favorite charity. If you miss the camaraderie of religious work groups and committees, and have time available, volunteer to serve at a local school, library, hospital, food pantry, historical society or any other organization that seeks to do good in your community. If you miss occasions to dress up and go out, get a small group together for regular excursions to shop or go to a restaurant, museum or theater. If you miss the table fellowship, plan your own pot luck dinners, coffee and dessert parties, or cocktail gatherings with a spread of hors d'oevres and wines. Consider joining or starting a book club or other activity group, or invite fellow hobby enthusiasts to start one with you. If you miss the music and literature of worship, open yourself to the world of the arts. If it's playing a role in shaping the world that you miss, get involved in politics, and consider running for office in your local or state government. If you miss Sabbath-keeping, plan rituals that will give you the pleasure of remembering one day a week to keep it holy in your own way.

And if you are concerned that major life events and times of transition must now come and go without formal recognition, in the next two chapters you will find rites, rituals and ceremonies to use as they are, or to modify to better suit your needs.

From my spirit to yours, all the best.

Chapter Seven: Private Rituals

MORNING

I greet this day with an open heart.
My path is sacred.
This moment is holy.

PILGRIMAGE

Barefoot and simple
    I come to this moment a pilgrim.
The blessing I seek lies within me.
    I am filled with my love,
    I am struck by my wisdom;
    I overshadow myself.
My spirit is sacred.
My life is holy.

COURAGE

I awake with a willing heart.
Today I will face hard challenges,
and I am afraid.
I draw strength from my silent spirit.
I gird my loins with love.
I am stronger than my fear.
I go forth on holy ground.

OUTDOORS

(adapted from Native American teaching)
Earth, my body:
I go forth on flesh of my flesh.
I am one with the earth.
Water, my blood:
I drink the life of my ancestors.
I am one with the waters.
Air, my breath:
I breathe the exhalations of life.
I am one with the air.
Fire, my spirit:
I am light; I am heat; I dance.
I am one with fire.

MID-DAY

I am here, now.
I see what is around me
    and within me.
I hear what is around me
    and within me.
My life is sacred.
This moment is holy.

DAY'S END

For all that went well, I am thankful.
For all my mistakes, I am sorry.
For what didn't get done,
    tomorrow will come.
Let dreams fill this holy night.

MIDNIGHT

Sleep has left me for now.
I hear the night sounds.
I shelter the sleeping world in my heart.
This place is sacred.
This moment is holy.

RECEIVING

As I breathe in, I receive peace...
   ...As I exhale, peace fills my mind.
As I breathe in, I receive love...
   ...As I exhale, love fills my heart.
As I breathe in, I receive healing strength...
   ...As I exhale, healing fills my body.
As I breathe in, I receive holiness...
   ...As I exhale, holiness fills my spirit.

GIVING BACK

As I breathe in, I receive peace...
   ...As I exhale, peace fills the world.
As I breathe in, I receive love...
   ...As I exhale, love fills the world.
As I breathe in, I receive healing strength...
   ...As I exhale, healing fills the world.
As I breathe in, I receive holiness...
   ...As I exhale, holiness fills the world.

OUTGROWTH

My heart is a garden,
  my thoughts are roots.
My words are flowers,
  my deeds are fruits.

GUIDED MEDITATION

Record the following in your own voice, with or without soft music, or learn it well enough that you can mentally guide yourself through it with eyes closed. Be seated comfortably. If outdoors, choose a spot where you can remain undisturbed for about twenty minutes.

- *Allow your muscles to relax comfortably.*
- *Find your vertical balance and settle in.*
- *Close your eyes.*
- *Follow the rhythm of your breathing.*
- *Give yourself permission to be right where*
    you are, right in this moment,
    letting go of thoughts,
    letting go of emotions.
- *Only be present to yourself*
    right here, right now.
- *This place is sacred and this moment is holy.*

- *Create a mental image of your surroundings.*
- *In your mind, visit each part of the scene until at last you find yourself sitting right where you are.*
- *Stay with the mental image of yourself, having no judgement, only acknowledging that this is where you are.*
- *Allow this image to fade away, as you turn your attention inward.*
- *You are calm.*
- *You are emptied, like a cup.*
- *Allow your spirit to speak, in what ever way that may happen for you.*
- *Allow your spirit to fill your cup, in what ever way that may occur.*
- *Sit in peace, letting the silence support you.*

[allow ten or more minutes]

- *Gradually become attuned again to your senses.*
- *Hear and feel what is around you.*

- *Know that the goodness you have experienced will remain within you.*
- *Breathe deeply.*
- *Let your eyes float open when you are ready.*

BRIEF MEDITATION

- *Sit comfortably. Relax your body.*
- *Soften the focus of your eyes as you gaze at a neutral focal point.*
- *Hear the sounds around you, then allow them to fade as you tune them out.*
- *Turn your attention to your breathing, letting thoughts drift away and emotions become still.*
- *Close your eyes.*
- *Imagine that you are drawing in peace from the earth beneath you, from the all that is above you, from everything around you.*
- *Let the peace fill you with quiet strength.*

   [sit in silence for a while]

- *Allow your eyes to drift open.*

Note: If at any time in your meditations an insight comes that alarms or worries you, it might be wise to talk it over with a trusted friend or counselor. Remember, though, that if you were tired, or under stress, it's possible that your imagination took the lead. Take what was good from the experience and release the rest.

Chapter Eight: Shared Moments

BABY NAMING CEREMONY

Welcome, friends.

On behalf of (_____ and _____), thank you to each of you for coming today. It matters very much to them that you're here to share in the happiness of this occasion.

We name our children in a public setting as a way of acknowledging that each child is a person in his or her own right.

A name provides an identity and a sense of belonging within a family and a community,

and it distinguishes each of us as an individual.

As we name this child today, each of you has an opportunity to consider the role you hope to play in (his/her) life.

And as you offer your support and encouragement,

>you serve as a living example to (_____),

>and help (him/her) to achieve (his/her) full potential.

(_____ and _____), please tell us the name

>that you have chosen for your child.

>(One or both parents: "_____ _____ _____")

Why did you choose that name?   (Parents reply)

(<u>Baby's First, Middle and Last name </u>), everyone here

>welcomes you, and wishes you a long life

>in a loving and peaceful world.

We hope you'll grow into a wise and compassionate

>person, fulfilled and happy in all you do.

May you love and be loved, and may you bring joy to

>all who know you.

(_____ and _____), taking

>responsibility for the well-being of a child

>is work that will change you forever.

It's a shared mission that will draw you closer together,

>and allow you to see and appreciate

>each other's strengths.

I invite you now to state your intentions as parents in the presence of those gathered here.

Do you intend to cherish (_____) throughout (his/her) life, so that (he/she) may always be confident in your love?   ["We do."]

Do you intend to do your best to protect and provide for (him/her), to guide and respect (him/her),

so that she may live in security and peace? ["We do."]

Do you intend to foster (his/her) creativity, curiosity and intelligence so that (he/she) may dream big and fulfill her potential?   ["We do."]

Hear these words from Kahlil Gibran's "The Prophet":

(A designated Friend or Family Member comes forward to read)

Your children are the sons and daughters
of Life's longing for itself.
They come through you, but not from you.
You may give them your love
but not your thoughts,
for they have thoughts of their own.
You may house their bodies
but not their souls, for their souls

dwell in the house of tomorrow, which
you cannot visit, even in your dreams.
You may strive to be like them,
but do not seek to make them like you.
For life does not go backward nor
tarry with yesterday.
You are the bow from which your children
are shot forth
as living arrows.

IF THERE ARE SIBLINGS PRESENT:

The arrival of a new child marks the beginning of a lifelong bond between siblings. (__Sibling's name/s__), you are an important part of welcoming this new baby, and making (him/her) feel right at home. (_____) is lucky to have a (brother/sister) like you, and we hope that you will be best friends forever. (Sibling name/s), do you promise to try your very best to love (_____) and to help (him/her) whenever (he/she) needs you?

You may say, "Yes, I promise."

["Yes, I promise."]

(Continue here if no siblings are present)

It has been said that it takes a village to raise a child.

(_____ and _____) are aware of the
    challenges that lie ahead, and they are so very
    grateful to have all of you as their extended
    family and circle of friends.

And so, on their behalf, I invite you all to respond to
    the following questions:

Do you intend to love (_____), and to hold
    (him/her) in your heart?   ["We do."]

Do you intend to share your time, your wisdom and
    your understanding with (him/her)?
            ["We do."]

Do you intend to support (_____ and
    _____) with your love, and to give them your
    guidance, reassurance and help as it may be
    needed in raising this child?   ["We do."]

(_____), it seems you're off to a great start in life.

All of these people love you very much.

We wish you good health, much happiness,

    and a bright future.

And now, please join me in a round of applause for

(_____ and _____),

[for (siblings' name/s, if any)]

and for baby (_____).

•

(A meal or refreshments may be shared.)

•

WEDDING CEREMONY

<u>Officiant</u> faces the gathering of family and friends at the center front, holding order of service and copies of the couples' vows. <u>Entry music</u> is played.

<u>Attendants/Witnesses</u> enter from opposite sides and walk toward the front, coming to stand on either side of the Officiant. If a <u>Flower Child</u> or <u>Ring Bearer</u> is used, they may lead the way for the <u>Intendeds,</u> who enter last. The <u>Intendeds</u> enter and stand side by side facing the <u>Officiant.</u>

Officiant: Friends, we are gathered together in this beautiful place, enfolded in the pleasure of each other's company, to witness and celebrate the joining together of [Intended One] and [Intended Two] in marriage.

We are here to surround them with our love, our hopes, and our best wishes in order to strengthen them for their life together as a married couple.

Marriage is the very model of love and mutual honor that we hope to see in all human relationships.

It is well-said that marriage is the foundation of human society.

And so, at this time, I ask each of you gathered here

to express your support for this union by
answering the following question:

Do you support this couple in marriage?
If so, please answer "I do."

<u>People:</u> "I do."

<u>Officiant:</u> [Intended One] and [Intended Two], this is a special day for you, for all of us who have gathered to celebrate it with you, and for many others who know and love you.

But neither I, nor these witnesses, can join you in marriage; only you can do that.

Only the two of you, living together in fulfillment of the vows you make today, can make of this marriage the union it is meant to be.

And so, I ask you now to commit yourselves, one to another. Please join your hands.

[Intended One], will you have [Intended Two] to be your [husband/wife], to live with [him/her] and cherish [him/her] in the bond of marriage? If so, please answer, "I will."

[Intended Two], will you have [Intended One] to be your [wife/husband], to live with [her/him] and cherish [her/him] in the bond of marriage? If so, please answer, "I will."

(Special music may be played or performed)

<u>Officiant:</u>   [Intended One], please make your promises to [Intended Two].
   (Officiant hands the vows prepared by [Intended One] to him/her).
   <u>*[Intended One]*</u> *reads vows*

<u>Officiant:</u>   [Intended Two], please make your promises to [Intended One]
   (Officiant hands the vows prepared by [Intended Two] to him/her).
   <u>*[Intended Two]*</u> *reads vows:*
<u>Officiant</u> *(recovers printed vows)*

(Special music may be played or performed)

[Intended One] do you have a ring for [Intended Two]?
   [ring is presented]
[Intended One] this ring is your gift to [Intended Two]. As you place it on (her/his) finger, please repeat after me: "[Intended Two], I give you this ring - as a sign and pledge of my undying love."

[Intended Two] do you have a ring for [Intended One]?
   [ring is presented]
[Intended Two] this ring is your gift to [Intended One].

As you place it on his/her finger, please repeat
after me: "[Intended One] I give you this ring --
as a sign and pledge of my undying love."

[Intended One] and [Intended Two], may these rings
serve as a strong symbol, both for you and for
the world, that you are bound to one another
in love.

[Intended One] and [Intended Two] in your life
together, may you freely give and receive love
from one another;

May you encourage each other in whatever trials may
befall you;

May you share each other's joys, and help each
other through difficult times.

May you grow to trust yourselves and each other, and
endeavor to always speak your truth in love.

May you show kindness to each other,
and may you create a home
which welcomes those in need,
and strengthens all who enter.

Dear Friends, it's with happy hearts that we conclude
this ceremony, and offer our hopes --
that [Intended One] and [Intended Two], may
enjoy an ever-deepening love,

and an abundance of years in which to fulfill the vows they have made here today.

[Intended One] and [Intended Two], you are now
> married according to my witness as Officiant,
> according to the witness of the loved ones gathered here,
> and according to the State of _____.

You may seal your vows with a kiss.
I now present
> [Intended One] and [Intended Two] [Last name]

(Recessional music is played)

•

(A meal or refreshments may be shared.)

•

WEDDING CEREMONY
Including a Child or Children
from previous marriage

<u>Officiant</u> faces the gathering of family and friends at the center front, holding the order of service and a copy of each of the couples' vows. <u>Entry music</u> may be played. <u>Attendants</u> enter and stand on either side of the <u>Officiant</u>. <u>[Intended One] and Child/ren, and [Intended Two] and Child/ren,</u> enter from opposite sides and walk toward the front, coming to stand in front of <u>Officiant.</u> The <u>Child/ren</u> may carry in the couple's rings tied on pillows, or basket(s) of petals or confetti to scatter.

<u>Officiant:</u> Friends, we are gathered together in this beautiful place, enfolded in the pleasure of each other's company to witness and celebrate the joining together of [Intended One] and [Intended Two] in marriage.

We are here to surround them with our love, our hopes, and our best wishes in order to strengthen them for their life together as a married couple.

And beyond this joy there is another -- for today we
>   witness not only the joining of a couple --
>   but also the binding together of a family.

For with this union, [Intended One]'s child/ren [name],
>   and [Intended Two]'s child/ren [name], will
>   become ["members of one family," "brother and
>   sister," "brothers," "sisters"]

[<u>Child/ren</u> may be seated]

<u>Officiant:</u> Friends, marriage is the very model of love
>   and mutual honor that we hope to see in all
>   human relationships.

It is well-said that marriage is the foundation of human
>   society. And so, at this time, I invite each of you
>   gathered here to express your support for this
>   union by answering the following question:

Do you support this couple in marriage?
>   If so, please answer "I do."

<u>People:</u> "I do."

<u>Officiant:</u> [Intended One] and [Intended Two], this
>   is a special day for you, for all of us who have
>   come to celebrate it with you, and also for
>   many others who know you and love you.

But neither I, nor these witnesses, can join you in
>   marriage;   only you can do that.

Only the two of you, living together in fulfillment of the vows you make today, can make of this marriage the union it is meant to be.

And so, I ask you now to commit yourselves, one to another. Please join your hands.

[Intended One], will you have [Intended Two] to be your [husband/wife], to live with [him/her] and cherish [him/her] in the bond of marriage?

If so, please answer, "I will."

[Intended Two], will you have [Intended One] to be your [wife/husband], to live with [her/him] and cherish [her/him] in the bond of marriage?

If so, please answer, "I will."

<u>Officiant:</u> [Intended One], please make your promises to [Intended Two]. *(Officiant hands the vows prepared by [Intended One] to him/her).* <u>*[Intended One]*</u> *reads vows*

[Intended Two], please make your promises to [Intended One] *(Officiant hands the vows prepared by [Intended Two] to him/her).* <u>*[Intended Two]*</u> *reads vows*

(special music may be played or performed)

Officiant *(recovers printed vows)*: [Intended One] do you have a ring for [Intended Two]?

Child: *(offers ring)*

Officiant: [Intended One], this ring is your gift to [Intended Two]. As you place it on (her/his) finger, please repeat after me:

"[Intended Two] I give you this ring --
as a sign and pledge of my undying love."

[Intended Two] do you have a ring for [Intended One]?

Child: *(offers ring)*

Officiant: [Intended Two], this ring is your gift to [Intended One]. As you place it on his/her finger, please repeat after me:

"[Intended One], I give you this ring --
as a sign and pledge of my undying love."

[Intended One] and [Intended Two], may these rings serve as a strong symbol for you and for the world that you are bound to one another in love.

[Intended One] and [Intended Two], in your life together, may you freely give and receive love from one another;

May you encourage each other in whatever trials may befall you;

May you share each other's joys, and help each other through difficult times.

May you grow to trust yourselves and each other, and
 endeavor to always speak your truth in love.
May you show kindness to each other and to your
 children, and may you create a home
 which welcomes those in need,
 and strengthens all who enter.
Dear Friends, it's with happy hearts that we conclude
 this ceremony and offer our hopes
 that [Intended One] and [Intended Two] may
 enjoy an ever-deepening love,
 and an abundance of years in which to fulfill the
 vows they have made here today.
[Intended One] and [Intended Two], you are now
 married according to my witness as Officiant,
 according to the witness of the loved ones
 gathered here,
 and according to the State of _____.
You may seal your vows with a kiss.
I now present [Intended One] and
 [Intended Two] [Family Name]
 and their child/ren [Name/s].

•

(A meal or refreshments may be shared.)

•

CRONING CEREMONY

Friends are asked beforehand to come prepared to share why the experience and wisdom of the honoree are important to them. A center table is set with a pillar candle which has been lighted, a bowl of tea lights, and a long butane lighter. The leader wears a purple shawl and has another ready to place around the shoulders of the honoree at the close of the ceremony.

Leader: Friends, this space is sacred and this moment is holy. Today we honor the women who brought us into this world, the women who raised us, who taught us, who were a sister to us by blood or friendship, and who helped us become who we are.

We honor the foremothers who came before our grandmothers, and the generations of girls yet to be born.

In the unity of the feminine principle, we are one.

And, today, we gather our hearts with a special intention to honor one of our own -- one who has demonstrated the wisdom, humor and forbearance that characterize a Wise Woman Elder, one who has earned our love and respect, and who has helped us

to become who we are.
That one is (_____ _____ _____).
She is ____years, ___months, and ___ days old.
(_____), we thank you for allowing us to honor you today.

Before we begin, I invite you all to take a moment to remember an older woman in your life: someone in her later years who befriended you and encouraged you.

Remember her clearly... see her eyes, her face, imagine her near you in this moment.

When you are ready, I invite you to take a small candle from the bowl and place it in her honor.

As I light the flame, please say her name.

[Lighting of tea light candles]

As we think about the marks the years left on those dear women, and have left on us as well, consider the words of this song by Peter Mayer:

[Play on a computer screen or read aloud: Peter Mayer, "Japanese Bowl"]
https://www.youtube.com/watch?v=qOAzobTIGr8

I'm like one of those Japanese bowls
That were made long ago
I have some cracks in me
They have been filled with gold
That's what they used back then
When they had a bowl to mend
It did not hide the cracks
It made them shine instead
So now every old scar shows
From every time I broke
And anyone's eyes can see
I'm not what I used to be
But in a collector's mind
All of these jagged lines
Make me more beautiful
And worth a much higher price
I'm like one of those Japanese bowls
I was made long ago
I have some cracks you can see
See how they shine of gold.

*

Older women, whose faces and bodies show the years, are known and honored in many parts of the world, by many different terms of respect.

They are consulted as tribal elders, and turned to for
> wisdom as their people work to keep all things
> in balance, and discern the ways of peace.

In some places older women are sen as ones who walk
> the horizon between this world and the next,
> and thus have knowledge of unseen things.

But we acknowledge also that in many cultures,
> including our own, older women may be viewed
> not with respect but with scorn, or worse,
> may not even be seen as whole persons.

Our culture is often blinded to its senior members by
> its bias toward youth and beauty and success.

Indeed, far from honoring the old women among us we
> have been guilty of naming them and shaming
> them as Old Biddy, Old Bat, Old Hag,
> Old Witch, Old Bag -- and of course, Crone.

The word "Crone" is a derogatory term.

It was apparently first used as an insult to older women
> in France during the Middle Ages.

The word at that time was "charoign," which comes
> from the Latin word, "caronia," and that word
> means the rotting flesh of a dead animal,
> or as we know it today, carrion.

So, a withered, cantankerous old woman living alone
> was kicked aside as "carrion."

The cruelty of this judgement is not lost on us:

her body may have been withered and stooped
from malnutrition, she may have been cross
from hunger, pain and loneliness.
The word used to describe her then, and which
survives in Western culture today, is "crone,"
Clearly the word crone was intended as an insult,
and of course there are many other words that
have been hurled at women and girls to
diminish the feminine soul --
in all the stages of her life.
So what do we do with this particular insult?
There are some women who remember the energy and
hope of the women's movement decades ago,
and they are rekindling that spirit today
in order to proclaim the dignity of aging.
In the pride that African Americans showed when they
struck back against prejudice, declaring,
"Black is beautiful,"
in that same spirit
women elders today are saying,
"Aging is beautiful."
They are saying "yes" to aging -- not as a sign of decay
but as a badge of honor.
They say, "It's true, our flesh is not what it once was,
but we are entitled to the dignity of personhood,
and the possibility of a certain kind of wisdom.

We are here to help the new generation see the past as
>   a context for the present --
>   and as a tool for envisioning the future."

*

Wise Women Elders rejoice in finding each other:
>   we claim our personal power, and we sit
>   together in peace.

Therefore, along with many others, today we claim the
>   term "crone" as a title of honor.

(_____), it gives us great pleasure to be
>   able to tell you what you mean to us
>   and to name the good things we hope for you.

Would someone like to begin?

>   *[Sharing words of appreciation]*

Leader: (_____), you have heard the words
>   of these women who love you.

Will you honor us with a few words of your own?

>   *[Honoree speaks]*

Leader: (_____), you truly are a Wise Woman
>   Elder, and an example to us all.

As a Crone myself, I bestow upon you the title of
>   Crone, and give you the color purple to wear,
>   the color of the crone, the color of wisdom.

May you continue to grow in power and wisdom.

>   *[Leader wraps purple shawl around shoulders of honoree]*

*Portion between asterisks may be omitted in subsequent ceremonies with the same group.

•

(A meal or refreshments may be shared.)

•

GRAVESIDE SERVICE

Dear Friends, on behalf of the _____
    family I want to thank you for coming today.
May peace be with us all in this holy hour.
We've gathered here in remembrance of

_____ _____ _____.

In losing HIM/HER, our hearts are heavy with a
    mixture of both joy and sorrow.
Our joy comes in celebrating everything that was
    good in _____, and in remembering
    all the reasons why we loved HIM/HER.
In holding and in sharing those happy memories we
    are filled with gratitude.

And yet, as we realize that HE/SHE is now gone
    from us, that we will not be able to make new
    memories with _____, nor speak with
    HIM/HER, nor embrace HIM/HER again,
    our hearts are broken with sorrow.
This mixture: of joy in happy memories, and sorrow
    in losing HIM/HER as part of the future,
    this is the very essence of grief.
It is good and right that we fully experience both
    aspects of grief, welcoming equally
    the laughter and the tears that come,

acknowledging the mixture of rejoicing and
regret, allowing the feelings of good fortune
in having had HIM/HER for a while
and the emptiness we feel in this loss.

These emotions are good and natural expressions
of the heart.

Friends, we know that grief is most easily borne
when it is shared.

And so, how very good it is that we have come
together today, doubling our joy,
and halving our sorrow,
as we celebrate _____'s life.

We know that we are not alone in our feelings, for
grief is a universal experience.

The poet Edna St. Vincent Millay protested the
injustice of death when she wrote:

> *I am not resigned to the shutting away of*
> *loving hearts in the hard ground.*
> *So it is, and so it will be, for so it has been,*
> *time out of mind:*
> *Into the darkness they go,*
> *the wise and the lovely.*
> *Crowned with lilies and laurel they go!*
> *But I am not resigned.*
> *Lovers and thinkers, into the earth with you.*
> *Be one with the dull, indiscriminate dust.*

A fragment of what you felt,
  of what you knew,
A formula, a phrase remains,
  but the best is lost:
The answers quick and keen,
  the honest look,
the laughter, the love —
They are gone.
They are gone to feed the roses.
Elegant and curled is the blossom.
Fragrant is the blossom.
I know. But I do not approve.
More precious was the light in your eyes
than all the roses in the world.
Down, down, down
  into the darkness of the grave
Gently they go, the beautiful, the tender,
  the kind;
Quietly they go, the intelligent, the witty,
  the brave.
I know. But I do not approve. And I am not resigned.

[special music may be played or performed.]

I would now like to offer these words of tribute to
_____'s life.   *[Leader shares tribute]*

If anyone else would like to speak , you are welcome
to do so now. *[friends and relatives share tributes]*

[special music may be played or performed.]

Today we acknowledge that the last chapter in the life story of _____ _____ _____
has been written.

HIS/HER story is now complete,
but we will continue to tell it.

HIS/HER spirit has rejoined the infinite energy which is its natural home.

HIS/HER earthly body is of no further use
to HIM/HER, and so it returns to the earth from which it came.

*[Coffin or urn may be positioned in final resting place;
Soil may be cast upon the coffin or urn, if being interred]*

Let's pause for a moment of silent reflection.

Please listen to these words of comfort from the poet Mary Elizabeth Frye:

> *Do not stand at my grave and weep*
> *I am not there. I do not sleep.*
> *I am a thousand winds that blow.*

I am the diamond glints on snow.
I am the sunlight on ripened grain.
I am the gentle autumn rain.
When you awake in the morning's hush
I am the swift uplifting rush
Of quiet birds in circled flight.
I am the stars that shine at night.
Do not stand at my grave and cry;
I am not there. I did not die.

[special music may be played or performed]

Dear friends, together we have born witness
    to the life of _____.
We have strengthened each another in the sharing of
    our sadness and our joy.
We have drawn comfort from each other through both
    smiles and tears.
And now we go forth from this place
    with tranquil hearts,
    remembering the one we have lost,
    and celebrating the love of those who remain.

Go in peace.

•

(A meal or refreshments may be shared.)

OTHER READINGS

Dear Lovely Death
Dear lovely Death
That taketh all things under wing
Never to kill
Only to change
Into some other thing
This suffering flesh,
To make it either more or less,
But not again the same
Dear lovely Death,
Change is thy other name.

By Langston Hughes

Mystery of Life
Before the sublime mysteries of life and spirit,
of infinite space and endless time,
we stand in reverent awe.
This much we know:
we are at least one phase of the immortality of life.
The mighty stream of life flows on,
and in this mighty stream we too flow on . . .
not lost . . . but each eternally significant.
For the spirit never betrays the one
who trusts it.
Physical life may be defeated but life goes on;
character survives,
goodness lives
and love is immortal.

By Robert G. Ingersoll

About the Author

Carol Maher lives in the Adirondack region of upstate New York with her husband Denny. She and Denny were born and raised in Sioux City, Iowa, and after nineteen moves in the course of fifty-two years of marriage, they are glad to be retired close to daughters Jennifer and Jill.

Prior to her career in ministry, Carol worked as a graphic designer and portrait artist. She has taught classes in portraiture, gourd art, calligraphy, and tole painting.

www.ingramcontent.com/pod-product-compliance
Lightning Source LLC
Chambersburg PA
CBHW072056290426
44110CB00014B/1713